Out on a Limb

- A Devotional Guide for Missionaries

Janet Dallman

PRESS

Out on a Limb
- A Devotional Guide for Missionaries
by Janet Dallman

Printed in the United States of America.

ISBN 9781498470919

www.xulonpress.com

Acknowledgments

To God for saving me, for giving me an interesting—if sometimes challenging—life and for helping me to write; I who was always bottom of the class in English!

To my husband, Peter, for his unconditional love, encouragement and support—both in everyday life and in the writing of this book.

To my parents for their love and example throughout my life and for their contribution to the unusual life I've led.

To all my friends and colleagues—both past and present—who have either knowingly or unknowingly helped me write this book. Thank you for sharing your lives and stories with me.

Out on a Limb—
A Devotional Guide for Missionaries

Contents

Preface

*F*irst things first; thank you for choosing this book. If you are working overseas, I pray that it will help, encourage and challenge you as you read the Bible and reflect on your life as a mission partner. If you are supporting someone who works abroad, I pray that this book will help you to understand and pray for your mission partner, as well as encourage and challenge you personally.

Those living outside their native country face unique challenges related to that calling, but also face all the challenges common to the human race, only in an unfamiliar context. I wrote this book to encourage Christian workers as they face struggles that can be hard for those at home to truly understand but also to help them deal with the difficulties that human life brings to all of us—wherever we live. This book is especially written with newer mission partners in mind, but I trust it will be a book to keep and dip into for a long time to come.

Second, allow me to introduce myself: I am a mixed up person! I am a British citizen with a Welsh father and an English mother, and I was born in the Democratic Republic of the Congo. I have so far lived in four countries—the Democratic Republic of the Congo, the UK, Senegal and Japan. I have worked with four different mission agencies—Wycliffe Bible Translators, BMS World Mission, Pioneers and OMF International. I am married to an Englishman, but we have now spent more of our married life in Japan than in the UK. We have worked field-side and home-side, in language study, student work, church planting, administration and pastoral care. Like many of you reading this, my true citizenship is in heaven, where I know I will finally feel fully at home.

With that in mind, I have written this book from my own perspective and experience—I can do no other. However, not all the experiences shared in this book are my own, but all are either true, or true to life. (All names have been changed.) You may find that some sections of this book will be more applicable to you than others, but I trust that as you read, you will be able to apply most of what I've written to your own context. I believe that the issues many missionaries face, while appearing different on the surface, are, at heart, much the same.

Finally, I have written this book with God's help and inspiration, but I know that I continue to fall far short of God's standards every day of my life. I continue to pray for his transforming power to be at work in my life, and I pray that his power might also be at work in you—even through this book, imperfect though this author most definitely is.

How to Use This Book

I would like to imagine you reading this book with a cup of something you like on hand, sitting in a comfortable and quiet place with your Bible and notebook beside you and a heart ready to hear and respond to God's voice.

Out on a Limb is designed as a book of devotional readings. Each devotion consists of stories and examples, Bible passages, application, an 'Interact' section and a prayer. You may choose to use this book daily, weekly or even periodically, whichever pattern suits you. Most importantly, try not to rush to read it and get to the end, without engaging with the issues it raises. You may choose to read the book in the order it is presented (the reasons for which are explained in the introduction), or you can read the devotions as seems appropriate to your current circumstances.

I would encourage you to set aside at least thirty minutes to read the text and to engage with some or all of the suggestions for inter- action. You may not find all the Interact suggestions helpful to you personally, but I have included a variety which I trust will be helpful to different kinds of people and in different situations. (It may some- times be appropriate to set aside more time or come back to the mate- rial more than once.) It would also be extremely helpful to keep a journal in which you can note how God has been speaking to you or things you want to do as a result.

Out on a Limb is a devotional guide, not an academic book, although I trust it will stand up to scrutiny. It is also necessarily short and much more could be said than there is space for here. Please use it as a 'jumping off place' for your own thoughts and reflections.

Ultimately, how you use this book is up to you and will be related to your circumstances. For example, having small children may mean that life is never quiet or unhurried! I trust that however you use this book, it will bring you help and encouragement even in the midst of dark or challenging times—those times when you feel 'out on a limb.'

Introduction

Out on a Limb is divided in to eight sections;

- Physical Challenges
- Spiritual Challenges
- Mental Challenges
- Linguistic Challenges
- Cultural Challenges
- Emotional Challenges
- Organisational Challenges
- Family Challenges

Each section is designed to focus on one particular area of the life of an overseas Christian worker. Some sections deal more with the practical or external aspects of living in a culture different to your own, while other sections are more about the internal aspects of what it means emotionally and spiritually to live and work overseas. However, each section is often a combination of both these aspects.

The sections have been arranged in an order that seems appropriate to me, particularly in terms of the physical challenges of setting up home or health issues—which generally come before dealing with some of the spiritual, mental or linguistic challenges. Cultural challenges also may not emerge at the beginning but spring up later. However, I recognise that any of these challenges can and do occur or re-occur throughout a mission partner's time overseas.

Physical
Challenges

Setting up Home

*J*ust this week, my husband and I and a team of helpers lugged furniture up the stairs and in to yet another apartment for new missionaries. The furniture has 'been around the block' a few times — to say the least. Part of our responsibility as those who welcome new missionaries to the field is to find and set up homes for them. Actually, it's rather fun and very satisfying to see a new home take shape and to embellish it with those small touches that can make all the difference.

Setting up home is a chore for some but is a joy for others. At the extreme ends of the scale, it can be done carelessly, or it can take up too much of our time. How do we and how should we set up home in a new country? How culturally adapted do we need to be in our personal living space? What things are essential for you and your family?

As we prayerfully consider this topic, we need to begin with our focus on Jesus, who said of himself, 'Foxes have dens and birds have nests, but the Son of Man has nowhere to lay his head' (Matthew 8:20). This was Jesus' response to someone who promised to follow him wherever he went. When we are obedient to Christ's call on our lives, it may mean that we also have literally nowhere to lay our heads. If that is the case for you, you are in the best company possible. However, for most of us, it is probably unlikely to mean that. Most of us are likely to have a space to call our own and to make our own. However, this phrase of Jesus should be a continuing challenge to us as we consider how much time and money we spend on making our space a home.

When Jesus sends out his disciples he says; 'Do not get any gold or silver or copper to take with you in your belts—no bag for the journey or extra shirt or sandals or a staff, for the worker is worth his keep' (Matthew 10:9–10). Although these verses specifically refer to a travelling ministry context, surely they also have something to say to those of us who live in more permanent homes. There is a sense of frugality here, of not living luxuriously, in these verses. Jesus also says; 'Do not store up for yourselves treasures on earth, where moths and vermin destroy, and where thieves break in and steal. But store up for yourselves treasures in heaven, where moths and vermin do not destroy, and where thieves do not break in and steal. For where your treasure is, there your heart will be also' (Matthew 6:19–21). Jesus knows how dangerous money and possessions are for us!

Sometimes, in order to cope with a new and perhaps frightening place, there can be a temptation for new missionaries to focus too much on home making. They can fall into the trap of spending too much time and money on things for their new home—that is, if such things are available to buy. (If those things aren't available, they may simply live life wishing they had—whatever it might be.) These words of Jesus are and should be a continuing challenge to each of us to live simply, buying what we need when we need it.

However, others can get carried away with austerity, need and practicality alone. Some folk can spend too little time and money on their new home, not really caring adequately for their own needs or for those of their family. It may also mean that their home cannot be a place of ministry to those around them. Think of how Jesus enjoyed hospitality at the home of Mary and Martha. God used their home to minister to others. The Bible tells us that God gives us everything we need for our enjoyment. He is not a mean, stingy God! We have a generous God—more generous than we can ever hope to fully understand (1 Timothy 6:17).

Long ago, as a short-term worker in Africa, I can remember wanting to buy an ice cream on a particularly scorching day. I can still remember feeling guilty about spending the money. However, I realised then what I still practise now; God delights to give good gifts to his children, and that includes the occasional ice cream! Matthew 7:11 says, 'If you, then, though you are evil, know how to give good gifts to your children, how much more will your Father in heaven give good gifts to those who ask him'!

Interact

1 Begin your time with God with thanks. Thank him for sending Jesus. Thank Jesus for living a rootless, homeless life on earth. Thank him also for all his good gifts to you and your family.

2 Ask God to show you if you have sinned in this area of possessions. Have you have allowed them to control you, rather than the other way around? Are your possessions or your home too important or not important enough? Confess your sins to him.

3 Ask God to show you how to live appropriately, simply and responsibly, yet also abundantly and generously in your ministry context.

Prayer

Lord, thank you that you love me so much that you sent Jesus to come to this earth to live, and to die for my sins. Thank you that you are a generous God in absolutely every sense of the word. Forgive me when I assume otherwise by my actions. Help me to get a balance between holding lightly to my home and my possessions but also to buy what I need, as well as being generous to those around me. It's a hard balance to keep, so I need your help. Amen.

When I Can't Get What I Want

'Have you got a red light I could borrow?' asked one new missionary as we drove her home from the airport. Pause. 'Sorry, could you say that again please?' 'A red light: I need it because I have a cold.' My husband and I exchanged glances. What was she talking about? As British people, the only 'red light' we know about is a dubious part of town! Another missionary of the same nationality helpfully explained that it was an infrared lamp, which people used to fight colds and other minor ailments. In Japan, we discovered, these machines are only used in hospitals and are fearfully expensive. No red light.

'Why can't I use my mobile phone from home?' asked another new missionary—rather indignantly. Try as we might to explain Japan's amazing mobile or cell phone system, it sounds rather unlikely to those who've never been here before. 'Japan just isn't like anywhere else. It uses a different system.'

'Why can't I buy 100 percent beef mince in the supermarket?' 'Why does the bank ATM charge to withdraw money outside banking hours?' 'Why does the Internet take that long to get connected?' 'I just want to be able to buy the kind of bread I'm used to.' 'Where can I buy a deodorant that will work for me?'

What can't you buy where you are? What home comfort are you hankering for? What doesn't work like you're used to in your home country? Japan is a highly developed country, and as missionaries here, we recognise how fortunate we are even to be able to ask what are in many ways such frivolous questions, but it still leads to frustration at the beginning. You may be in a country which offers far less materially, and you will no doubt experience some level of frustration about what isn't available to you.

However, this need to get what we want doesn't stop in the beginning stages of missionary life, nor is it solely about possessions. It continues but in different ways. What about when we can't get our own way in a ministry decision? What about when no one else sees it our way? What happens if the mission requests you to take on a ministry you didn't want or plan? It is sad to say, but very often we don't respond well when we can't get what we want. Sometimes, we revert to the childish way of relating; 'that's not fair!'

> I am not saying this because I am in need, for I have learned to be content whatever the circumstances. I know what it is to be in need, and I know what it is to have plenty. I have learned the secret of being content in any and every situation, whether well fed or hungry, whether living in plenty or in want. I can do all this through him who gives me strength. (Philippians 4:11–13)

Paul says, 'I have learned . . .' twice in two verses! This 'being content thing' is not automatic. It doesn't come right away. It is a *learnt* behaviour. I find that encouraging. It is something that all of us need to learn — and re-learn. The clue to learning contentment is found in verse 13, 'I can do all this through him who gives me strength.' If God is with us and is working in us by the power of his Holy Spirit, he can help us learn contentment.

Bear in mind also these words from Hebrews; 'Keep your lives free from the love of money and be content with what you have, because God has said, "Never will I leave you; never will I forsake you"' (Hebrews 13:5). Once again, the writer affirms that we can be content *because* God has promised never to leave us or forsake us. Surely, that's the key. We have God's presence with us — what more do we need?

'The fear of the Lord leads to life; then one rests content, untouched by trouble' (Proverbs 19:23).

Interact

1 What do you want, but can't get right now? Tell God about it.
2 Do you need to confess the sins of pride, self-righteousness, inflated ego or greed?
3 Ask God to help you learn contentment. Ask him to so fill you with his Holy Spirit and to give you satisfaction with him, that all your other needs and wants pale into insignificance.
4 Reflect on Psalm 131;

My heart is not proud, LORD,
my eyes are not haughty;
I do not concern myself with great matters
or things too wonderful for me.
But I have calmed and quietened myself,
I am like a weaned child with its mother;
like a weaned child I am content.
Israel, put your hope in the LORD
both now and for evermore.

Prayer

Lord, I confess that my heart is often far from content. Please forgive me for my sins against you—of pride, greed, self-righteousness and inflated ego—and help me to change. Please fill me afresh with your Holy Spirit and raise my eyes to see all the good things you have already given me and want to give me simply by your presence and your work in my life. Please calm and quiet me: may I be like a weaned child, content with you. Amen.

Staying Healthy

*H*ave you met missionaries who never seem to stop working, who don't have days off and who barely take holidays? I'll bet you have. Perhaps you struggle with this, too. Or perhaps you've realised that you aren't making time to eat well. Meal preparation is done in a rush, with little thought given to nutrition and much thought given to time-saving. Perhaps you always seem to be ill since becoming a missionary? It happens. Stress and change, new bugs and overwork can all play a part.

Perhaps you struggle with exercise—doing it I mean, not the broad concept! You're not a sporty type, you don't enjoy it and you aren't motivated to do it. I find myself in this category. What about sleeping? I write as one who kept my parents on duty throughout the night as a child and who hasn't improved a great deal as I've got older. Do you have healthy sleeping habits?

A good starting place to consider physical health and well-being is 1 Corinthians 6:19–20; 'Do you not know that your bodies are temples of the Holy Spirit, who is in you, whom you have received from God? You are not your own; you were bought at a price. Therefore honour God with your bodies.' Although these verses come at the end of warnings against sexual immorality, they can equally apply to the subject of caring for our health.

Your body is a temple of the Holy Spirit. That blows me away just thinking about it. Even though 2 Corinthians 4:16 tells us that '. . . outwardly we are wasting away, yet inwardly we are being renewed day by day.' God's Holy Spirit lives in these sometimes

broken bodies, these 'jars of clay' as Paul calls them in 2 Corinthians
4. That is a truly staggering thought. Think on that for a moment. Not
only that, I do not belong to myself: I belong to God. He has bought
me with the precious blood of Jesus. It cost God more than I can ever
know or understand to buy me back for himself. My body is on loan
to me. It is being used by God now for his purposes.

If God bought us at such great cost and sacrifice to himself, and if
he lives in our bodies by the power of his Holy Spirit, we had surely
better look after these bodies! God has planned in rest for his people.
'Six days you shall labour and do all your work, but the seventh day
is a sabbath to the Lord your God. On it you shall not do any work .
. .' (Exodus 20:9–10a). We need a day of rest: God designed us that
way. How good are you are taking that day? And if you do take it,
how well do you use it? When we were new missionaries, we spent
five days a week in language study, one day at church, with one day
for rest. I won't forget the dressing down we received from our medical advisor when she discovered we spent our day of rest doing the
shopping, washing, cleaning, writing letters and so on! Another missionary wisely said; 'Rest is part of the work.' How are you doing in
this area of your work for God?

How are you doing on eating well? While our bodies are only
earthly tents (2 Corinthians 5), they are *useful* earthly tents in God's
purposes. Of course, God can use anyone in any state of health for
his glory if they are submitted to him, but if you are going to stay
in mission for the long haul, you need to eat well. You need to think
about mundane things like fruit and vegetables, vitamins and fibre.
I have known several missionaries who seemed to try to live on
Japanese *obento*, or lunch boxes. Generally, these box lunches are
of a high standard, but they don't provide all the body needs and can
sometimes contain unhelpful additives.

Exercise: Paul tells Timothy, 'For physical training is of some
value . . .' (1 Timothy 4:8). How can you incorporate more exercise
in to your daily routine? Can you walk somewhere locally, or join
a local sports club, if your community has such a facility? Is there
someone with whom you could exercise regularly—which might
help both of you to get and stay fit for the work God has called you to?

In addition, God has designed our bodies to need sleep, and we need to make sure that we get enough of it. How can you make sure you get adequate sleep each night? Finally, let me close with John's words to Gaius in 3 John 1:2, 'Dear friend, I pray that you may enjoy good health and that all may go well with you, just as you are progressing spiritually'.

Interact

1   Have you sinned in the area of caring for your body or caring for the physical needs of your family? If so, confess these things to God and take time to list up what needs to change.
2   How can you live more healthily in your work patterns, your rest, exercise, your eating habits and your sleeping habits? Write down concrete ways to improve in these areas?
3   Choose one area to work on particularly over the next month. Share that with a friend or prayer partner and ask them to help you achieve it.
4   Are you struggling with health issues? Do you need to see a doctor? Examine your heart and take steps to care for your 'jar of clay' (2 Corinthians 4:7).

Prayer

Lord, I confess my weaknesses in the area of caring for my health and that of my family. Please help me to prioritise not just my time with you but also my physical needs. Forgive me when I don't do that and give me the strength to change where I find that difficult. Amen.

Security and Conflict Situations

*A*rrested on their honeymoon! That's what happened to one missionary couple in Congo in the late 1960s. My own parents got married in the midst of a Congolese army mutiny, unable to go on honeymoon—bags packed ready to leave at thirty minute's notice. Another occasion found our house surrounded by soldiers. No one knew why. A group of petrified missionaries and children were escorted by soldiers to Sunday school, but by lunchtime the soldiers had gone, with no explanation.

Perhaps you live in a similar situation? The army, the insurgents and the rebels are volatile. Perhaps you live in the shadow of terrorism? As I write, there have been three terrorist attacks in Pakistan and one in Nairobi. Perhaps where you live, low-level civil unrest grumbles on, leaving you jumpy and on edge?

Or perhaps you work in a country which is closed to 'traditional mission'? You have to be extremely careful who you meet and what you say. You can't even share with your supporters what is really going on or where you really are. You know that you are under suspicion.

How should we react in such situations? Psalm 37:1–7 tells us;

> Do not fret because of those who are evil or be envious of those who do wrong; for like the grass they will soon wither, like green plants they will soon die away. Trust in the LORD and do good; dwell in the land and enjoy safe pasture. Take delight in the

LORD, and he will give you the desires of your heart.
Commit your way to the LORD; trust in him and he
will do this: he will make your righteous reward shine
like the dawn, your vindication like the noonday sun.
Be still before the LORD and wait patiently for him;
do not fret when people succeed in their ways, when
they carry out their wicked schemes.

First, let's examine what we are *not* to do in such situations. We
are told, 'Do not fret' — twice. I don't know about you, but I usually
need telling at least twice! The word 'fret' means to suffer emotional
strain. It is an on-going concern, hovering in our minds. Imagine
a fretful child: this is not how God's people are to behave. Why?
Because, the Psalmist tells us, those who do wrong will wither and
die. Their fate is already determined, and they will not succeed. God
knows, and he will deal with it.

So, what *are* we to do?

Trust in the LORD — Simple to say; hard to do. I think it means
living each moment in prayer, giving everything we are and do into
his hands. 'Trust in the Lord with all your heart and lean not on your
own understanding . . .' (Proverbs 3:5a). Trusting in the Lord is the
opposite of leaning on our own understanding. Even when we can't
make any sense of what is going on, we can commit it into God's
safe hands.

Do good — Such a simple phrase. What good do your hands find to
do? Do it in Christ's name!

Dwell in the land and enjoy safe pasture — Does this mean that we
will be kept physically safe in every situation? No. We all know of
some who have lost their lives in the service of Christ. Some com-
mentaries suggest that these words mean living faithfully. If we live
lives of faith, we are already dwelling in his land and will enjoy his
safe pasture, even if the physical or political situation around us is
far from safe or secure.

Take delight in the LORD—This phrase conjures up pictures of a child's face enraptured at a Christmas gift, or a couple gazing at each other on their wedding day. We need to be those who don't simply trust, but those who delight in God. For some of you, this will come more naturally, but others of you may struggle. We need to be so focused on God that all else around us pales in to insignificance.

Commit your way to the LORD—We are called to hand over our plans to God, to depend on him, to place everything entirely in his hands. This is an on-going and absolute trust in his sovereignty and reliability.

Be still before the LORD—Are you good at being still? I'm not, and I suspect many of you are the same. We are not to be those who run around like a chicken with its head cut off! We are commanded to be still before God.

Wait patiently—This is as hard as being still! Picture the child on Christmas Eve who can't wait to open his presents. Although the word isn't used in this particular passage, Japanese has a very helpful word when it comes to waiting. It is *machinozomu*: *machi* means 'wait' and *nozomu* means 'hope.' As God's people we can wait, filled with hope, because God is always faithful.

Interact

1 What situation are you facing? Write in your journal about your feelings and fears.
2 Confess any areas of worry or sin to God and receive his forgiveness.
3 Mediate on Psalm 37 or 1 Peter 3:8–16.
4 Ask God to help you trust in him and commit yourself in to his hands—no matter what happens.
5 What 'good' should you be doing in your current situation? Take some practical steps to do those things.
6 Ask God to help you not simply to trust in him, but to delight in him.

7   Ask God to help you to be still and to wait for him.

8   If your situation is potentially life-threatening, pray and talk with others for God's way forward. Do you need to leave, or is God calling you to stay?

Prayer

Lord, you know that I am frightened for myself and for my family. I don't know what's going to happen, but thank you so much that you *do* know. Help me to make you my ultimate security. Please help me to trust you every minute of every hour. I commit my ways to you again today. In the power of your Holy Spirit, I choose to turn consciously from worry and place everything in to your hands. Help me to do good today—even to those who threaten me—so that I can live in peace and honour you no matter what happens. Help me to delight only in you, to be still and to wait for you to act. In the name of Jesus, amen.

Disaster!

*W*here were you on 11 March 2011? My husband and I were in the city of Sapporo, northern Japan as the awesome tsunami drowned countless thousands further south—many of whose bodies have never been found. Can you still see those terrifying scenes of water rushing over sea walls, fields, streets, houses and people? I can. Do you remember the earthquake in Haiti on 12 January 2010 and the utter devastation brought to such a desperately poor nation and her people—220,000 estimated dead. Or what about the Indonesian tsunami on 26 December 2004? The thousands of people swept away, homes obliterated and vast swathes of land 'pickled' with salt water—ruined for years to come. Perhaps you remember Typhoon Haiyan and floods in the Philippines in 2013? Or forest fire? Or famine?

How should we react to disaster? How do we cope when our personal equilibrium is shattered—or to put it more plainly, when we are scared stiff? Do we stay put? Do we run? Psalm 46:1–3 tells us: 'God is our refuge and strength, an ever-present help in trouble. Therefore we will not fear, though the earth give way and the mountains fall into the heart of the sea, though its waters roar and foam and the mountains quake with their surging'.

A colleague of mine always had a fear of moving from the north of Japan to live and work in the vast, sprawling metropolis of Tokyo. Tokyo, sitting as it does on the 'ring of fire' is particularly prone to earthquakes—large and small. It experiences many imperceptible wobbles every day. However, bigger shakes occur regularly, although by-and-large the trains merely stop temporarily before continuing on their super-efficient journey through the maze of criss-crossing urban train lines of Tokyo.

These lines from Psalm 46 gave my friend hope and courage that God would be her refuge, her ever-present help in trouble. And even if the mountains—and indeed, even if the heart of Tokyo were to fall into the sea, she had no need to fear. I pray that these verses can give you hope and courage, too, as you face whatever disaster has befallen you, or the country in which you live. May God be your refuge and your ever-present help in trouble. If you are living in fear of disaster, then allow these verses to soothe your soul and bring balm to your mind.

Second, how should God's people respond in disaster? Micah 6:8 tells us: 'He has shown you, O mortal, what is good. And what does the LORD require of you? To act justly and to love mercy and to walk humbly with your God'. We are called to reach out to those who are suffering with the love of God in Christ. What this looks like in practice, however, will be as different as each disaster and the people affected, are to one another.

After the Japanese earthquake and tsunami, many mission agencies and Japanese believers throughout Japan poured in to the affected areas to offer practical relief—clear up, clean up, open soup kitchens, and give out rice, vegetables, noodles, fruit, clothes—all the practical needs of life. However, along with those practical gifts, they also took the time to listen to those who wanted to share their stories, such as the man who escaped by climbing a tree and clinging on for dear life! Or the lady whose husband is now bedridden because he can't face life after the triple disaster. Only later did those volunteers seek deliberate opportunities to bring the good news of Jesus Christ to those whose lives had been devastated in just a few hours.

What you do in your area and in your situation will be different, but we are called to do something. What will it be?

Interact

1   What disaster are you facing—or what possible future disaster distresses you?

2   Talk with God about that by writing in your journal or composing a poem.
3   Write your own prayer of trust, or if you can't do that just yet, write a prayer to express how you feel right now.
4   Pray and ask God to show you how you need to show mercy to his people in this disaster situation.

Prayer

Thank you, Lord, for the wonderful promise in Matthew 28, that if we are doing your work, you will be with us always, to the very end of the age. Help us to remember that promise as we face disaster. Thank you that nothing that can happen on this earth can ever change the solid fact that you are our refuge and strength and our ever-present help in trouble. Praise you! Help us also, Lord, to know how you want us to be involved in reaching those overwhelmed by disaster with your love in practical, pastoral and spiritual ways. Help us to be bold, knowing that we have not been given a spirit of timidity, but of power, love and self-discipline (2 Timothy 1:7). Amen.

Spiritual Challenges

Obedience and Submission

$\mathcal{M}$any in the West are brought up to be independent. From birth, the process to separate from parents begins. Parents are keen to wean their babies and to put them in their own bed, in their own room. Children are encouraged to develop their personality and to be their own person. Young people are stimulated to develop their thinking and reach their own conclusions. Students are challenged to think independently and to live intentionally.

My husband and I have worked in Japan for many years, where they seem to view things rather differently. Child-rearing is less about encouraging independence and more about training a child to live appropriately within a certain community. This may mean that the child is not always encouraged to do their own thing, but rather is encouraged to consider others in the group and the consequences of their actions on those people.

One system strongly values independence. The other system values submission to the community as of prime importance. Neither style of upbringing is all right nor all wrong, but both styles have helpful as well as less helpful points. However, I do wonder sometimes if those brought up in a more independent way can have problems as they consider submitting to God's will for their lives.

When I first arrived as a new missionary in Japan, I had submitted to what I believed was the will of God for my life, but I had not done it graciously! I had made the physical sacrifice of going to Japan. I was there in body, but not in mind. Around that time, I picked up a dusty, old book in the OMF library called *Green Leaf in Drought-time* by Isobel Kuhn. It is the biographical story of Arthur and Wilda

Matthews set in 1953, after the communists had come to power and all the missionaries were forced to leave China. I came across the following quote:

> A few nights later it came to Arthur like a flash: the Son had left Heaven, not *submitting* to the will of God, but *delighting* in it. Up to now they had been submitting; rather feverishly submitting ... They had been acting like servants who don't want to do it but have to, because they can't get out of it. What a different attitude was the Son's! (1)

God spoke to me very powerfully as I read these words and considered my own situation as a frustrated, homesick language learner. These words also described my attitude. The book goes on to say of God's yoke; 'The yoke is *light* only as it is *taken*, and not as it is *suffered*'. (2) I was definitely *suffering* under God's yoke. I was challenged to submit to God's will for my life whole-heartedly, not to suffer his will half-heartedly. I was able to turn a corner that day in my early missionary walk.

Hebrews 12:9 challenges us to submit to God, our Father, in everything—no matter how tough: 'Moreover, we have all had human fathers who disciplined us and we respected them for it. How much more should we submit to the Father of spirits and live'.

James 4:7 says, 'Submit yourselves, then, to God. Resist the devil, and he will flee from you'. I needed to submit, willingly and whole-heartedly to God's will for my life, which, for me, meant being a missionary to Japan. I confessed my sin of a disobedient heart within my outward physical obedience.

Deuteronomy 30:11, 14–18 says:

> Now what I am commanding you today is not too difficult for you or beyond your reach ... No, the word is very near you; it is in your mouth and in your heart so that you may obey it. See, I set before you today life and prosperity, death and destruction. For I command you

today to love the LORD your God, to walk in obedience to him, and to keep his commands, decrees and laws; then you will live and increase, and the LORD your God will bless you in the land you are entering to possess. But if your heart turns away and you are not obedient, and if you are drawn away to bow down to other gods and worship them, I declare to you this day that you will certainly be destroyed. You will not live long in the land you are crossing the Jordan to enter and possess.

These verses encouraged me that the work God had given me to do was not too difficult for me. Learning Japanese, living in Japan and being a missionary here would be demanding, but it was not too difficult or beyond my reach. It also challenged me to live obediently, knowing that obedience brings blessing and disobedience leads to separation from God and ultimately death.

Interact

1 Prayerfully examine your life before God and ask him to speak to you.
2 List any areas that he highlights in which you have not or are not being obedient.
3 Confess these things to God.
4 Ask God to help you to be obedient and submissive to him.
5 Thank God that he is with you and will help you, and that what he has given you to do is not too difficult for you.

Prayer

Lord, forgive me for my rebellious heart. I'm not happy living in rebellion toward you. Please help me to want your will more and to live in it. I cannot do it alone. Please change my heart, Lord, and help me to decide to love you, to obey you and to take your yoke upon myself delightedly. Thank you that what you've asked me to do is not too difficult for me or beyond my reach, otherwise you wouldn't have asked me to do it. Lord, I rely on you to help me live in obedience to you. I ask this in Jesus' name. Amen.

Honesty

*E*lderly Mrs. Suzuki handed us a creepy-looking, papier-mâché Japanese mask, saying, 'I thought you'd like this'. We both took one look at it and decided instantly that we didn't want it at all! However, what could we say? It's hard to refuse a gift in any culture, but in a gift-giving culture like Japan, it's even harder. After arriving home with our dubious 'gift,' we chatted about what to do with it. To be honest, it wasn't pretty, and it definitely looked suspicious. Was it even occultic in some way? We'd been given good luck charms before—was this another? Or was it simply an old Japanese mask used for drama?

We set out to investigate. After hearing our dilemma, long-standing Christian and member of the church leadership team, Mrs Takahashi, said that it was probably perfectly innocent and that Mrs Suzuki had just wanted to show kindness. OK, so the mask was above-board, but we still didn't want to keep it. Home assignment was coming up, and it wasn't worth storing for a year, but neither did we feel we could use it for display, so eventually and rather guiltily, we threw it away.

A week or two went by and life and packing for home assignment continued. One day, out of the blue, Mrs Suzuki telephoned and said that if we didn't want the mask, she would like to give it to her daughter. Help! What could we say? I'm sorry to have to tell you that we lied. But that lie didn't sit well with us, and we knew we needed to confess the truth to kindly Mrs Suzuki. I am more grateful than I can say that Mrs Suzuki graciously forgave us for both our lack of appreciation of her gift and our lack of honesty. (She had, in fact, guessed that we didn't like the mask and was trying to help us by taking it back.) God forgave us, and so did Mrs Suzuki. However, we learnt a very valuable lesson—again. Honesty.

The question of honesty comes up in all our lives in many different guises. How do we set our budget, so that it covers what we *need*—but perhaps not what we *want?* How do we claim expenses for extra costs, be that phone calls, flight costs, postage and so forth? How do you react when the policeman wants a bribe? Many missionaries, too, are left to manage their own time and resources. What shape does your working day take? Are you putting in the hours you know you should?

Do we act honestly and honourably in our relationships with others? Recently, I made a request of a co-worker and couched it as a favour, when in reality I was demanding what I wanted. I wasn't honest in my communication. On other occasions, we may need to be challenged to be more honest and open in communicating those things which are affecting us or our families—things that might often be considered private. If you are struggling with ill health or depressive thoughts, for example, it will affect your life and ministry, and it is important for colleagues and leadership to know those things. Of course, we need to share these issues appropriately, but it is far better, surely, to be honest about your struggles in order to receive support and understanding.

As Christians we serve an honest God. Numbers 23:19 tells us; 'God is not human, that he should lie, not a human being, that he should change his mind. Does he speak and then not act? Does he promise and not fulfil?' Honesty reflects God's character, and honest and honourable living—or the lack of it—affects our walk with Jesus. If we are living dishonestly, Satan will do everything he can to destroy us from the inside out. If we allow such sin to go unconfessed and unforgiven, we are heading for trouble!

> Therefore each of you must put off falsehood and speak truthfully to your neighbour, for we are all members of one body. 'In your anger do not sin': do not let the sun go down while you are still angry, and do not give the devil a foothold. Anyone who has

been stealing must steal no longer, but must work,
doing something useful with their own hands, that
they may have something to share with those in need.
(Ephesians 4:25–28)

Do not give the devil a foothold. Confess right away. Come clean.

Second, not only does our honesty or lack of it affect our walk
with Jesus, it also affects our witness in the name of Jesus Christ.
'Live such good lives among the pagans that, though they accuse you
of doing wrong, they may see your good deeds and glorify God on
the day he visits us' (1 Peter 2:12). May our honesty in the name of
Christ be attractive to unbelievers.

We are called to be holy and honest. We are called to reflect
God himself.

Interact

1   In what areas of your life are you struggling to be honest right
now? Confess these to God and receive his forgiveness.
2   What do you need to do to put things right? Make plans to do
just that and ask God for his courage and his help.
3   Think and pray about how you can be more honest and open
in your communication with those around you.
4   Affirm your desire to keep a clean slate with God so that you
can be used by him to share his wonderful news with those
around you.

Prayer

Lord, forgive me. I fall in to the trap of lying so very easily. Please
forgive me—not because of who I am, but because of who you are.
Thank you that you are faithful and just to forgive my sins and to
purify me from all unrighteousness. Thank you so much! Help me
to think carefully about how I communicate with people. Help me
to manage my finances and time in ways that honour you and are a
witness to all around me. Amen.

Going on or Giving Up?

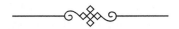

*I*s it all too much for you? Is each day such a struggle that you wonder how you will make it? Are you fed up with language learning, culture learning, your mission or organisation—just add the word which applies to you! Have you been criticised? Is your work is unappreciated?

Writing today is a struggle for me because it's one of those days when it's really tempting simply to walk away. Instead I've committed to writing a portion of this book. How can I write when I want to walk away from messy relationships, cultural misunderstandings and petty problems? There are days and times when we are all tempted to give up. Jack it in. Throw in the towel. What do we do at those times?

Hebrews 6:10–12 says;

> God is not unjust; he will not forget your work and the love you have shown him as you have helped his people and continue to help them. We want each of you to show this same diligence to the very end, so that what you hope for may be fully realized. We do not want you to become lazy, but to imitate those who through faith and patience inherit what has been promised.

God has not forgotten your work. God knows you've slaved in the kitchen all day to make food for that church event. God knows your brain is fried from stuffing it full of vocab. God remembers the time you've spent praying about a challenging situation. God knows your heart for your colleague who's driving you insane. God has not forgotten. God is not unjust. God knows the love you show for him. Let your heart be warmed and encouraged by these words from Hebrews.

These verses also tell us that we are called to be diligent—to the very end. We are to keep going, not to give up. We are called to do the work God has given us carefully, attentively and without getting sloppy. 'Keep on keeping on.' Boy! That's a tough calling! What do you need to keep on doing diligently today and every day? Ask God to help you: you surely can't do it otherwise.

We are also encouraged to copy the faith and patience of those believers who've gone before us and of those who are around us. Who do you know who has faith and perseverance in service that you can learn from? Is it your pastor? A senior colleague? A friend in your home country? Consider whose example you might imitate. Perhaps it would help you to get in touch with them to talk and ask for their prayers, that you might persevere in God's work, love, faith and patience.

There are times in all of our lives when we want to walk—or even run—away, but God calls us to keep on placing one foot in front of the other. When we first arrived in Japan, I cannot count the number of times I told my husband that I had to leave Japan. I just couldn't figure out how to do it honourably! We had been sent off by our supporting churches with prayer and financial sacrifice—everyone knew we were to be missionaries. We would have had to face the pressure and shame if we gave up and returned home. It was a desperate time for me, and I thought up some pretty desperate schemes. However, God challenged and encouraged me to keep going through these verses and others in the book of Hebrews.

However, there may come a time when God does call us to move on to something else in faith. Perhaps your family is growing up, and you need to consider new schooling options for them. Perhaps your parents are aging and beginning to need more care. Perhaps you sense a nudge at your elbow toward a different ministry. Perhaps you or your spouse is unwell.

There is a massive gulf of difference between giving up and running away, and in moving on to a new walk of faith. But how do we know the difference? A long time ago, someone told me not to make a decision to leave because something was difficult, but rather to make a decision to leave because God was calling you on to something else. It can be very easy to get our feelings confused if things are tough-going but much better to make a positive decision to get involved in a new place or ministry.

Interact

1   Wanting to chuck it all out the window? Talk to God about it. He understands.
2   Try writing a poem or a prayer about how you feel.
3   If you need to, make a deliberate decision to forgive someone who has hurt or is hurting you.
4   Thank God for his 'remembering.'
5   Ask God for his Holy Spirit to help you keep on putting one foot in front of the other, to be diligent in your service of him.
6   Consider who you might talk or pray with, whose faith and perseverance you admire.
7   Consider if your feelings are less about running away, and more about moving on to something new. Talk to God about it.

Prayer

Lord, please help me today. It feels like no one understands or appreciates me. It feels like what you've asked me to do is just too hard. But thank you that you remember: you know what I have done and do, that which no one else sees. Thank you that you are not unjust. Please help me to keep following you. Give me courage to persevere. Give me some sign of your encouragement today. And Lord, keep my heart open to you. Help me to keep listening to you—to stay or to move on. Help me to hear your voice clearly today and every day. In Jesus' powerful name, Amen.

Spiritual Warfare

'*S*atan is tenfold more of a reality to me today than he was in England'. So said Amy Carmichael, well-known missionary to India who first served in Japan. (3)

As a missionary to Japan, I can echo that statement. However, I am also a missionary kid, who was born in the Democratic Republic of the Congo and I used to be a short-term worker in Senegal. In Africa, there are charms just about everywhere you look; good luck amulets around the neck and charms of protection along the edges of the fields. There are witch doctors, and there are curses. However, what I hadn't realised before I came is that the same is true in the fast-paced, technologically-advanced, highly sophisticated country of Japan. There are 'sacred' trees, 'sacred' mountains, charms in wallets and handbags and on the front door, god shelves in shops and businesses, and charms in the car. Now that was unexpected!

When my husband and I first began to be involved in church planting, we realised the extent of the spiritual battle in Japan. We also realised that the devil tells the same lies all over the world. He may 'dress them up' in different clothes, which suit the culture, but they are still the same lies.

We came across church attendees who always fell asleep the moment the sermon began. Japanese people are known for hard work, but always falling asleep just at that point? We came across otherwise healthy new believers who felt physically sick on Sunday mornings every week. We came across people who experienced *kanashibari*—a rigid binding of the whole body. The medical explanation for this phenomenon is sleep paralysis, but some believe it is oppression by evil spirits. I encountered a lady who saw balls of light moving through her flat. She sensed evil, and I and another missionary were asked to pray for God's cleansing and protection. We came across a Christian whose old charm in a cupboard in her home caused her a distinct sense of uneasiness each time she walked past it. She eventually went through her cupboard with her home group, found the charm, threw it away in the name of Jesus and was set free. I've known missionaries who've had repeated nightmares, and I myself have awakened sensing evil. Was it my imagination? I can't say for sure, but I don't think so.

I hadn't come across this sort of thing much before I came to Japan. I was forced to re-evaluate my theology on spiritual warfare, and it wasn't very comfortable! (By the way, I am still re-evaluating and haven't necessarily come to firm conclusions.) I didn't want to exaggerate the devil's work, but I couldn't ignore some of these experiences, and I needed to learn how to deal with them.

When faced with some of these things I don't understand and haven't experienced, 1 John 4:4 always gives me both confidence and comfort; 'You, dear children, are from God and have overcome them, because the one who is in you is greater than the one who is in the world'. The one who is in me—Jesus Christ, by the power of his Holy Spirit—is greater than he who is in the world. I have Jesus! What a comfort in times of fear, what confidence in times of battle.

Likewise, Luke 11:21–22 says 'When a strong man, fully armed, guards his own house, his possessions are safe. But when someone stronger attacks and overpowers him, he takes away the armour in which the man trusted and divides up his plunder'. Jesus is the stronger man, and I know him! He alone has the power to overcome the devil and win the victory. Praise God!

When we are faced with unbelievers who are bound by spiritual oppression or believers who struggle to be free from their old lives or when we ourselves struggle to deal with evil forces, we need to remember that Jesus lives in us, and he is the stronger man. We have comfort and victory!

However, we also need to pray for God's protection. The forces of evil are real and powerful. We underestimate them at our cost, and at the cost of those we seek to serve. Matthew 6:13 says, '. . . lead us not into temptation, but deliver us from the evil one'. We must be bold in our prayers for ourselves and for those among whom we work.

Ephesians 6:10–18 says:

> Finally, be strong in the Lord and in his mighty power. Put on the full armour of God, so that you can take your stand against the devil's schemes. For our struggle is not against flesh and blood, but against the rulers, against the authorities, against the powers of this dark world and against the spiritual forces of evil in the heavenly realms. Therefore put on the full armour of God, so that when the day of evil comes, you may be able to stand your ground, and after you have done everything, to stand. Stand firm then, with the belt of truth buckled round your waist, with the breastplate of righteousness in place, and with your feet fitted with the readiness that comes from the gospel of peace. In addition to all this, take up the shield of faith, with which you can extinguish all the flaming arrows of the evil one. Take the helmet of salvation and the sword of the Spirit, which is the word of God. And pray in the Spirit on all occasions with all kinds of prayers and requests. With this in mind, be alert and always keep on praying for all the Lord's people.

Interact

1   In what ways have you seen or felt the devil at work in your life? Examine yourself before God, confess your own sins and renounce any evil influence in the name of Jesus.
2   In what ways have you seen the devil at work in the lives of those around you? Can you identify specific people or situations? If so, tell God about them and commit them to him.

3   Remind yourself that you are in Christ, he is in you and he is the stronger man—you have the victory!

4   Pray for yourself, for God's protection and his armour, but also for God's Holy Spirit's power to flow out from you to those around you.

5   Pray for God's power to overcome in any people or situations where you sense the devil at work.

Prayer

Thank you, Jesus, that by the power of your Holy Spirit, you are alive in me. Thank you that I am on your side, and you are on mine! Forgive me when I give the devil a 'foothold' in my life through my own sin. Set me free from Satan's power at work in my life. Cleanse me by your purifying Holy Spirit. Protect me from evil, and may I bring your light and peace to those around me. Amen.

Mental
Challenges

Independence and Dependence

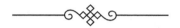

'*And* he said: "Truly I tell you, unless you change and become like little children, you will never enter the kingdom of heaven. Therefore, whoever takes the lowly position of this child is the greatest in the kingdom of heaven"' (Matthew 18:3–4). Jesus is explaining the upside-down values of his kingdom to the disciples. Greatness in God's kingdom is not about high position; it is about becoming like a child.

In the same way, when you become a missionary in a country foreign to you, with a language and culture you don't understand, you are forced to become like a child once again. Most children are happy enough being children—it is their natural lot and they accept that reality. Not so for adults who are suddenly forced to take on the role of a child, after years of living perfectly happily and independently as an adult! Losing control of your life is upsetting and stressful!

As a brand new worker to Japan, you can read nothing, write nothing, say nothing and understand nothing. If you've never learnt characters before, you can't even look things up in a dictionary. All those things you could do quite expertly in your home country, you can do no longer. You can't buy a stamp. You can't tell salt from sugar. You can't use the washing machine. You can't sing in church. Your competence and independence is rudely stripped away. You become like a child all over again. How about you—what can't you do?

What did you do before you became a missionary? Were you a doctor? A lawyer? Do you have a PhD? Did you run a successful business? Most missionaries are well-educated and highly intelligent people. In a sense, that's a given. Missionaries need to have good sense, a solid education and an ability to learn. If they didn't, they would struggle to be missionaries. Not only that, the mission field of the world doesn't need people who aren't good at what they do. The big snag, however, is that people, who are clever and good at what they do, struggle to become children again; they struggle to let go of their independence. Going back to school—whether literally to language school—or being thrust in to the school of life in another country is extremely tough.

However, these verses in Matthew should challenge us again; '. . . unless you change and become like little children, you will never enter the kingdom of heaven'. One of the characteristics of small children is their dependence on their parents. A two year old can't get a job to earn money. Three year olds can't make good decisions about the grocery shopping. Babies don't do the family laundry. Although as children get older, they may and probably should help with some of these things, children live dependent on their parents. The tragedy we see in our world and perhaps even around you, of children living off their wits and on the street is not how God designed the world to be. Babies and children were designed to need a family and to be dependent on that family.

As members of God's family, we are designed the same way. John 15:5 tells us; 'I am the vine; you are the branches. If you remain in me and I remain in you, you will bear much fruit; apart from me you can do nothing'. We are designed to walk with God, to be dependent on God. It can be a temptation for us to try and go it alone, but we're not designed that way and lasting fruit isn't borne that way.

In the same way, if you have joined a mission or a church, you don't have to—and shouldn't try to—go it alone. God has given you a new family to help you in your new situation where you are help- less! Of course, there will be a natural grief about your lack of ability and your loss of independence, but instead of focussing on that, let me encourage you to see this process, that of becoming a child again, in a positive way, rather than a negative way. Ask for and accept the help that is offered to you. You have a special chance to be on the receiving end from your brothers and sisters.

As a short-term worker in Senegal, West Africa, I worked as a secretary for the mission's branch director. He always signed his letters *interdependently yours*. That impressed me. That's what it's all about to be part of God's family. We are to be interdependent. This is your chance to need someone else; maybe later you will also be needed by another missionary.

Interact

1 Picture in your mind your child, or a child known to you. Watch them be what they are and do what they do. Ask God to speak to you about what it means to become a child again, dependent on the Father and on others.
2 Ask God to show you if your independence, or your intelligence, is getting in the way of what he would like to do in you and through you. Confess those sins to him.
3 Meditate on John 15 and ask God to speak to you through it.
4 Consider what help you have already received from brothers and sisters in Christ and make a point of thanking them for it.
5 Consider what help you still need and think about who you might ask.
6 Consider who might need your help, and how you might offer it in the most helpful way.

Prayer

Thank you, Lord, that you designed me to walk with you as my Father. Thank you that this gives me great assurance, comfort and freedom. But, Lord, you know how I hate not being able to do even the simplest things in my new environment! Please help me to swallow my pride and to become like a child again. Please work in me and through me to produce your heavenly fruit. May I be dependent on you and interdependent with my brothers and sisters. In Jesus' name, amen.

Humility

> Therefore if you have any encouragement from being
> united with Christ, if any comfort from his love . . .
> Do nothing out of selfish ambition or vain conceit.
> Rather, in humility value others above yourselves, not
> looking to your own interests but each of you to the
> interests of others. (Philippians 2:1a, 3–4)

*H*umility doesn't ever come easily to sinful human beings, but perhaps humility comes even less easily to strong-minded missionaries!

Christian workers are passionate about what God has called them to do—and so they should be. What higher calling is there than to fulfil the purposes of God and bring salvation to the lost? Absolutely none. However, sometimes the very passion, enthusiasm and call new missionaries have to reach people with the good news of Jesus, can blind them to their own weaknesses, sin and need for help and advice. Perhaps a few examples would help.

Phil was young, a relatively young Christian and newly married. He was highly intelligent with a couple of degrees. He knew God's call and was well trained. However, Phil struggled to submit to authority. Phil wanted things all his own way. Or take Jane. Jane had excellent language skills, had already lived in the country before becoming a missionary and had a vision to reach people for Christ. But Jane struggled to submit to authority. Jane wanted things all her own way.

These verses in Philippians are a massive challenge for any Christian, of any age, in any walk of life. However, we must also allow them to be a challenge to us in our work as missionaries. Let me ask you; do you consider others better than yourself? Do you look not only to your own interests, but also to the interests of others? I don't just mean the people you've come to serve, but the people you serve *with?* Sometimes our passion for those we have come to serve can damage those we serve with. Do we listen to those in our team? Do we give attention to those in authority over us? Are we willing to seek and take advice?

I like *The Message* translation of these verses;

> Don't push your way to the front; don't sweet-talk your way to the top. Put yourself aside, and help others get ahead. Don't be obsessed with getting your own advantage. Forget yourselves long enough to lend a helping hand. (Philippians 2:3–4 MSG).

Are you pushy? Are you self-centred, or your-ministry-centred, over those of others? How easy do you find it to 'forget yourself'?

If we are honest with ourselves, we can all hold up our hands and confess to the sin of pride. We wouldn't put it quite so bluntly, but to some extent or another, we all believe that we know best. We do. Admit it. An older single missionary told me about her experiences in Africa. When she first arrived, she found she was always being asked to pray for other missionaries' road trips and childbirth. What was this strange obsession with travelling and birth? Perhaps she would have focused on other things in prayer. Wisely, however, she kept quiet, and she soon discovered that travelling on the roads and giving birth were the two most dangerous activities for missionaries at that time! Praying for God's protection in these situations was right and good. Although she had been frustrated and felt she knew better, she realised her mistake.

In my own experience, my husband and I were leading a church plant in our second term in Japan, while the senior missionaries were on home assignment. We had worked with them in the church for two years, and we knew the church members well. However, the burden of leading a new church, full of almost all brand new Christians, with only two years of ministry experience and still-struggling language ability was extremely heavy. We could have asked for help from those with more experience, but we didn't. We didn't for a number of reasons, but one of the bigger reasons we didn't ask for help was pride. We did manage to hold the church together, but at great personal cost. My husband developed depression and eventually we had to leave the field and were gone for two and a half years. By God's grace we were able to return, but when we did, our personal resolve was to make sure we asked for help when we needed it.

None of us knows it all or can do it all. Ask for help. Take advice.

Proverbs 11:2 says, 'When pride comes, then comes disgrace, but with humility comes wisdom'.

Interact

1   Think through the different areas of your life: language study, ministry opportunities and home life. Ask God to show you any aspects of your thinking in each of these areas where humility is lacking. Confess these areas of sin to God, and delight in his forgiveness.

2   Think about what it means to 'clothe yourself' with humility daily. How can you do that practically? (See Colossians 3:12; 1 Peter 5:5.)

3   Cultivate an attitude of life-long learning and not simply in language and culture study. What can you learn from older missionaries, national believers and non-believers? Consider what questions you would like to ask and of whom. Make a plan to speak with them about these things.

4   Is there anything you are particularly struggling with right now? If so, share that with a friend, pastor, senior worker or prayer partner. Admit your need and share the burden.

5   Ask yourself how you can serve the body of Christ, rather than your own interests? That might be serving the local

church, your home church or your fellow workers. Take practical steps to do those things.

Prayer

Lord, please forgive my sins of self-sufficiency, self-reliance and pride. I confess these to you now. Please help me to be like Jesus, who made himself nothing, who humbled himself and became obedient to death. Lord, I have a long way to go. Please work in me by the power of your Holy Spirit. Please help me to clothe myself with humility, in the same way that I put on my physical clothes each day. Help me, too, to develop an attitude of learning from others and of serving others. In Jesus' name, and for his glory, amen.

Asking Questions and Taking Advice

*A*s a new mission worker I hope you've been asking lots of questions. It's part of your job description. How will you learn unless you ask? My father, once a missionary to the Democratic Republic of the Congo, spent one year in Belgium learning French before venturing to Congo itself. Having chosen to learn Welsh, rather than French, at school, Dad had to begin with the basics. He loved to tell the story of how he asked question after question of his exasperated linguistics teacher. That teacher thought Dad was daft because he asked so many questions! But guess who got top marks in the final exam?

Questions are vital to learning. However, here are two types of questions we can ask:

Curious Questions
Critical Questions

Curious Questions are simply fact-finding questions. For example, 'why do the traders in many African markets want to have a conversation with me before we start bartering for potatoes?' The questioner is simply trying to understand the culture in which they live. Their attitude is one of humility and wanting to learn.

Critical Questions, on the other hand, can be loaded with cynicism, negativity and a lack of trust or belief. An example might be; 'why do African market traders always have to talk about their family before we can get on?' The questioner is not asking for information, but expressing anger or disbelief at what they see as annoying. Their attitude is one of pride and not wanting to learn.

The difference is clear. What sort of questions have you been asking?

Second, when you've asked your question, do you really listen to the answer? Hopefully, if you adopt a humble attitude of learning, then you will listen and act on the answer you receive. However, all too often it is easy to ask questions out of pride, anger and a lack of trust. When we do that, it is much harder to listen to the answer, to take advice or to act positively on what we hear. 'Listen to advice and accept discipline, and at the end you will be counted among the wise' (Proverbs 19:20).

2 Chronicles 10 tells us about a man who asked for advice — from two different sources. Jeroboam came to King Rehoboam and pleaded with him to have mercy on the Israelites and release them from the harsh labour to which they had been subjected under King Solomon. Rehoboam wisely takes time to consider his decision and ask for advice. First, King Rehoboam asks the elders who had served under his father Solomon for their advice. They advise that if he shows kindness, the people will always be his servants. However, we are told that Rehoboam rejected the elders' advice. Instead, he asked those who had grown up with him and who served under him for their advice. They encourage Rehoboam to inflict yet further suffering on the Israelites. One result of Rehoboam's mistake is recorded in 2 Chronicles 10:19; 'So Israel has been in rebellion against the house of David to this day'. The second result is in 2 Chronicles 12:15b; 'There was continual warfare between Rehoboam and Jeroboam'.

It's good to ask honest, humble, curious questions, but we must ask them of the appropriate people, and we must listen to their answers! Who can and should you be asking questions of in your situation? 'In the same way, you who are younger, submit yourselves to your elders. All of you, clothe yourselves with humility towards one another, because, "God opposes the proud but shows favour to the humble"' (1 Peter 5:5).

Interact

1   Take time to consider whether you ask *curious questions* or *critical questions*. Ask God to show you the truth about your heart.

2   Confess those occasions when you know that your heart has been critical, unbelieving, disrespectful, negative or untrusting.

3   Thank God for his forgiveness and ask him for humility to learn and to accept advice.

4   Consider who you might go to for help and advice. What makes this person appropriate?

5   Consider the words of 1 Peter 5:5 and Hebrews 13:17 and how they apply to you and your situation.

Prayer

Thank you Lord for the inquisitive mind you have given me. Help me to question what I see and listen honestly and openly and, above all, with humility. Help me to develop a learning attitude. Help me to ask for advice from appropriate people and to receive it willingly — as from your hand. In the name of Jesus, amen.

Linguistic Challenges

Moses Moments

Terry despaired that he would ever learn Japanese. He worked hard and did his homework, but he didn't seem to be making progress. After an especially frustrating language class, Terry returned home utterly dejected. He was never going to be able to speak Japanese. (Can you relate to these feelings—whatever language you're learning?)

After lunch Terry settled down to his quiet time. Turning to Exodus 4, when God had called Moses to speak about the release from captivity of his people, Terry began to read. You know the story: it is when Moses expresses his own inadequacies to the Lord. Finally, in verses 10-12 Terry read;

> Moses said to the LORD, 'Pardon your servant, Lord.
> I have never been eloquent, neither in the past nor
> since you have spoken to your servant. I am slow of
> speech and tongue.' The LORD said to him, 'Who
> gave human beings their mouths? Who makes them
> deaf or mute? Who gives them sight or makes them
> blind? Is it not I, the LORD? Now go; I will help you
> speak and will teach you what to say.'

Terry was amazed! In the same way God spoke to Moses, God was speaking to him! Terry could also say that he was 'slow of speech and tongue.' He was a quiet man, softly spoken and he spoke slowly. But the Lord's words to Moses gently rebuked Terry. 'Who gave human beings their mouths? Who makes them deaf or mute?' Terry realised once again, what of course he already knew: God gave him his mouth, and God alone could enable him to speak or cause him to be mute.

God's promise to Moses was, 'Now go; I will help you speak and will teach you what to say.' Terry knew that God was speaking to him. *God* wanted him in Japan. *God* would help him to speak, and *God* would give him the words to say. Encouraged at God's knowledge of his situation, as well as God's power at work within him, Terry settled down to his language homework once again.

Accounts of God either enabling speech or causing people to be mute are not uncommon in the Bible. Zechariah's unbelief at the news of a son led to a nine-month period of silence (Luke 1:20). However, in response to his obedience, it says, 'Immediately his mouth was opened and his tongue set free, and he began to speak, praising God' (Luke 1:64). Or consider the story of Balaam and his donkey in Numbers 22:28 that says; 'Then the LORD opened the donkey's mouth . . .' Balaam then proceeds to hold a conversation with his faithful steed! If God can open a donkey's mouth, he can certainly help you learn to speak whichever language is causing you headaches!

Mark 7:31–37 gives the account of Jesus' healing of a man who couldn't hear and could barely speak. It says of Jesus, 'He looked up to heaven and with a deep sigh said to him, "Ephphatha!" (which means, "Be opened!"). At this, the man's ears were opened, his tongue was loosed and he began to speak plainly' (Mark 7:34–35). These verses can encourage all you Terrys or Moseses out there. We belong to Jesus. Jesus is the Word of God (John 1:1). Jesus, the Word of God, opened this man's mouth by his miraculous power. In the same way, he can also help you. He can open your ears to be able to hear and understand. He can open your mouth to enable you to speak this new language. Be encouraged: you belong to and worship a God who speaks and who enables us to speak.

Finally, consider Pentecost in Acts 2. Verse 4 says, 'All of them were filled with the Holy Spirit and began to speak in other tongues as the Spirit enabled them'. Now be honest, which of you hasn't wished for a divine gift of tongues in the area of language learning?

However, the Bible is clear that this gift of language was given by the Holy Spirit to those to whom he chose to give it. It had nothing to do with the believers, but was all of God. In the same way, God by the power of his Holy Spirit may choose to give us this gift in our new language, but more often than not, he chooses to give us the gift of *struggling to learn*. This too is a gift, though it might not be the one we would choose! However, God can give the gift of tongues—both permanently and on particularly needful occasions.

At 10.30 pm one night, we received a phone call summoning us to the bedside of a desperately ill elderly lady who wished to believe in Jesus and receive baptism. At that point we still struggled a lot with language and leading a church plant for the first time, so we wondered if we were really up to the job. When we reached the hospital, we tried to confirm the lady's belief in Jesus. It was difficult to hear her and to understand, so much so that I had to place my ear next to her mouth. However, what she said clearly conveyed her firm belief, so we baptised her with the sign of the cross on her forehead. It was only afterward in talking to her daughter that we discovered that I was the only one to have understood this lady! I was not then and am not now, a leading speaker of Japanese, but I can testify that God enabled me to hear and understand that night, by the power of his Holy Spirit.

Be encouraged! God can open your ears and your mouth. Jesus is the Word of God. God sends his Holy Spirit on his people. All you need to do is to be obedient to the calling you are given. Pray and have hope!

Interact

1   Confess your sin of doubt, if you need to, and know that God forgives you.
2   Ask God to open your ears and your mouth and to fill you with his Holy Spirit in order that you may learn the language.
3   If you're artistic, design a banner or poster with the verses from Exodus 4 on it to remind yourself daily of this truth.
4   Make a study of how God enabled his people to speak for him in the Old and New Testaments.

5   If you need to, think through a study plan to help you focus
on your language learning. What time of day will you study
and for how long? How can you take your language learning
forward from this point?

Prayer

Lord, speak to me, that I may speak
In living echoes of Thy tone;
As Thou hast sought, so let me seek
Thy erring children, lost and lone.

—*Frances Ridley Havergal 1836–79*

Lord, that is my prayer. Please keep me close to you; please fill me
with your Holy Spirit and enable me to hear and speak your words
after you. Thank you that you are all powerful and can speak through
me—whether or not my language is perfect. Help me today to trust
you for my language ability, but help me also to work hard at it for
your glory and not my own. In Jesus' name, amen.

Comparison

*S*he was just so infuriatingly good at Japanese—and what's more she'd arrived at language school three months after I had! She didn't seem to agonise over transitive and intransitive verbs, sentence particles or pronunciation. She was clever and confident. I felt like a lumbering elephant; inadequate and pathetic. Over time, the gap between our language skills widened until a huge gulf seemed to separate us.

I grew to resent her ability, her confidence—and even her, herself. This lady, who was in the same position as me, a similar age to me and someone who had been my friend, became an enemy to be beaten! That small seed of jealousy had taken root and had grown into full flower until it strangled the friendship between us. Oh, I don't think she ever knew—I think I hid it pretty well—but *I* knew. I knew too that jealousy, envy or covetousness is sin. The Bible condemns it. Way back in Exodus 20 it says; 'You shall not covet your neighbour's house. You shall not covet your neighbour's wife, or his male or female servant, his ox or donkey, or anything that belongs to your neighbour' (Exodus 20:17).

If you will permit me, allow me to paraphrase that for language learners;

> *You shall not covet your colleague's language learning ability. You shall not covet your colleague's cultural understanding and appreciation, or anything else that they seem to have but you do not.*

The issue of comparison also calls to mind the parable Jesus told about the talents a master entrusted to his servants in Matthew 25:14–30. Each servant received a different amount of talents. The first two set to work at once to increase the money given to them, but the final servant simply buried the money. The first two servants were praised for their faithful service and given greater responsibility and security, but the last was condemned as wicked and lazy, and ultimately was thrown out.

When it comes to mental ability and aptitude, we are all formed differently by God, and all he makes is good. Some of us have the ability to reach the heights and excel in language learning—like a hot air balloon floating high in a cloudless blue sky. Others of us are destined to scrape along the sea bottom! The point, of course, is not what ability you have. Whatever you have or don't have is given by God, and he thinks it's perfect for you. The point is what you do with what you have. Will you be like the servants who went to work at once and invested wisely, or will you be like the one that buried even the smallest talent he had in the ground. God does not hold us accountable for what we are *unable* to do, but only for what we *are able* to do. If we work hard with what he has given us, he is pleased. He doesn't compare his children.

A Japanese missionary talking about his language ability when he was struggling with his English once quoted Proverbs 30:8–9:

> Keep falsehood and lies far from me; give me neither poverty nor riches, but give me only my daily bread. Otherwise, I may have too much and disown you and say, 'Who is the Lord?' Or I may become poor and steal and so dishonour the name of my God.

He then re-phrased it to say something like this;

> *Lord, give me neither poverty nor riches in language learning, but only what I need for each day. Otherwise, I may become proud of my own ability and disown you and say, 'Who is the Lord?' Or I may despair and disown the name of my God.*

70

These thoughts encouraged me enormously as I continued to struggle with learning a highly complex language and culture. What are you struggling with? What I needed—what we all need—is to rely on God for his strength and ability. Ultimately, it's not about the verb declensions or cultural adaptation, important though these are. It's about doing our best with what we've been given and relying on God for his help.

Interact

1   Have you ever felt the temptation of comparison? You may have been tempted to take pride in your own abilities, or you may have been tempted to despair. Either is damaging and sinful. Confess these feelings and struggles to God and receive his forgiveness.
2   Ask God for his joy in who he made you to be, in those around you, and in your relationships.
3   Pray to receive God's strength to resist temptation in the area of comparison. Ask him to help you to work to the best of your ability and yet to rely on his strength alone.

Prayer

Lord, I confess that I so easily fall into the dangerous pit of comparison. I recognise before you just how dangerous it is. Lord, please forgive me and help me to know your pleasure as I use the gifts you have given me to the very best of my ability. Help me to rely on you for everything, including language and culture learning. Help me also to move forward and to gain fluency in the language you've given me to learn. In Jesus' name I pray, amen.

Church Life

'*W*ell, I didn't get any of that!' I muttered angrily after church one day. 'I have absolutely no idea what the pastor was saying! I mean what on earth is the point of even going to church if I can't understand a word, and I can't talk to anyone, either?'

'Well,' explained my patient husband, 'he was talking about faith and the peace that it brings to our lives or something like that'.

'How could you ever make that out?' I exploded.

'Well, I heard the word "faith" at one point, and then "peace" and I think he was talking about life as a Christian, so that's probably about right', said my husband, showing off his superior listening comprehension skills and good guesswork.

During our orientation in steamy Singapore before going to Japan, we were told that there are two types of language learners. Those that need to understand approximately 60 percent of the content before they feel they understand what is being said; and those that need to understand a whopping 90 percent before they can follow the conversation. Guess which sort I am? Which sort are you, I wonder?

I confess that my attitude about going to church on Sunday became less godly with every passing week! Sundays fast became my least favourite day. This went on for months, even years. I came out of church way less holy than when I went in. My husband used to say he could almost see the steam coming out of my ears as we sped home from church on the train.

I knew I was sinning with my angry thoughts, but I didn't know what to do about it. Eventually, God spoke to me, and I drew up what

I called 'The Church Depression Emergency Kit.' I commend it to you if you are struggling in a similar way. The aim is to be able to be positively and spiritually involved in the service and the church fellowship—even though you may understand very little.

- Pray for the pastor
- Pray for the Sunday school or youth leaders
- Pray for those sitting either side, in front and behind you
- Pray for any non-Christians attending the service
- Pray for the impact of the sermon in the hearts of those who hear it
- Sing along with the songs—as you are able—and try to remember the words in your own language if appropriate
- Read the Bible passages for yourself in your native language (I found I could often work out what the passages were, even if I didn't understand what was being said about them.)
- Plan your own sermon or talk on the passage being preached—what would you say? Ask God to speak to you.

Using this tool transformed my attitude about church in the early years. Of course, it was still far from easy, but it meant I could make a positive difference by being there, and it also meant that God could still speak to me. Hebrews 10:24–25 are verses that God used to speak to me a lot earlier in my life (and if we ever meet, ask me and I'll tell you that story), but they are also applicable here;

> And let us consider how we may spur one another on toward love and good deeds, not giving up meeting together, as some are in the habit of doing, but encouraging one another—and all the more as you see the Day approaching.

There is also great power, I believe, in the ministry of 'presence', simply standing shoulder to shoulder with our brothers and sisters in Christ. We may not understand what is going on, but we can be there supporting them with our presence and our prayers.

Interact

1   What's church like for you? Write in your journal or write a prayer about your feelings.
2   Confess any sinful attitudes if you need to.
3   What can you do—in fact, what will you do—to get involved and engaged in your current church situation? Make a list. You can borrow from mine or write your own.
4   How can you encourage spiritual vitality in your own life, even though you aren't getting much or only very little from the church service?
5   Pray for your church and yourself to grow in 'knowledge and depth of insight, so that you may be able to discern what is best and may be pure and blameless for the day of Christ, filled with the fruit of righteousness that comes through Jesus Christ—to the glory and praise of God' (Philippians 1:9).

Prayer

Father God, thank you for all the expressions of diversity in your church worldwide. Thank you that you delight in the worship your people bring—poor though it is by the standards of heaven. However, Lord, I confess to you now that I am struggling to worship in the church I am in. Lord, please transform my heart, my mind and my will to worship you in all circumstances and to enjoy the diversity of your family worldwide. Amen.

Boredom, Demotivation and Lack of Progress

*L*esley had arrived six months previously, raring to go, and began learning language and culture with enthusiasm and success. However, more recently she'd had to re-learn some of those verb forms from the first few months, and she'd begun to feel rather bored. It didn't really feel like she was making much progress at all.

Richard was a gifted evangelist and speaker and had come to the field 'on fire' for the lost. But now he was now stuck in language school and made a fool of himself whenever he went to market! Why was all this taking so long: he was an intelligent man, after all? Not only that, his home church was apt to ask him how many converts he'd made. How could he tell them the truth?

Keith was a church planter. He had plenty of experience and good language ability. He prayed a lot and believed he was following the guidance God had given him. But nothing was happening! No matter how many leaflets he and his small band of believers delivered, no matter how many prayer walks he made or how many evangelistic courses the small church ran, nobody had come to faith in the last year.

Lorraine was in a remote location with a team who were translating the gospel of John. The hours of painstaking work in the baking heat, with little forward progress, bumping up against linguistic nightmare after nightmare, was hardly what she imagined her life would be like as a missionary.

Can you relate to one or more of these individuals? You began well, but now you're bored, demotivated and discouraged at the lack of progress.

'Since, then, you have been raised with Christ, set your hearts on things above, where Christ is, seated at the right hand of God. Set your minds on things above, not on earthly things' (Colossians 3:1–2). These verses can bring us back in balance. 'You have been raised with Christ', says Paul. Wow! 'Raised with Christ'. Let that phrase sink in a moment. No matter how you are feeling today, you have been raised with Christ! All too often, we allow our *feelings* to dictate our lives, rather than relying on the *facts* of our salvation. We have been raised with Christ. Today, when you are bored, demotivated and discouraged, remember and live out the truth of your resurrection with Christ.

'Set your hearts on things above'. If you're anything like me, you won't find it easy to obey this command. This, however, is a decision of the will. We are to make a daily, moment-by-moment, conscious decision to concentrate on the 'things above'. The *Living Bible* puts it this way, 'Set your sights on the rich treasures and joys of heaven . . .' *The Message* translation puts it like this;

> Don't shuffle along, eyes to the ground, absorbed with the things right in front of you. Look up, and be alert to what is going on around Christ—that's where the action is. See things from his perspective. (Colossians 3:1-2 MSG).

What a great and oh-so-accurate description. All too often we shuffle along, eyes to the ground, absorbed with the things right in front of us. We appear like an elderly person, bent nearly double, struggling to walk on an uneven pavement or sidewalk. What are your eyes on today? Learning vocabulary? Writing a sermon? Making sure the kids to do their homework? These are all good things, but they are not to be our ultimate focus, says Paul. We are to be those who 'look up,' those who let heaven fill our thoughts. Instead of shuffling along, we are to appear as an Olympic runner, whose whole body is poised and ready for action, whose eyes are focused on the goal.

Interact

1   Meditate on the phrase, '. . . you have been raised with Christ'. Make some notes on how this should be affecting your life in general and your life today in particular.
2   Bring God your disappointments and discouragements. Ask him for his grace to bear them and for his power to be at work in them.
3   Confess to God your sin of 'shuffling,' rather than 'sprinting.' Imagine him lifting your chin and straightening your back and showing you his glory.
4   Ask God for his direction, his help and his re-energising power to be at work in your life.

Prayer

Lord Jesus, thank you that I have been raised with you. Help me to live today in the light of that. Lord, you know that I haven't found things very easy recently. Please give me your comfort, encouragement and the motivation to continue moving forward. Please raise my eyes heavenward and strengthen my 'run' of faith. I ask this for your sake and for your glory, amen.

Cultural
Challenges

Culture Chameleon?

'I bought the white coat because it blends better in Japan,' said one of our new missionaries. She was absolutely right. Brighter colours are becoming more common in Japan, but muted pastels, beige, grey and black are still seen more frequently.

Some aspects of a new culture are attractive to us. In Japan, the beautiful gardens, the exotic kimonos, the intricate stationery, the politeness and service are all attractive to me. They are uniquely Japanese, and I enjoy them. However, some aspects of our new culture cause us to struggle. In an outburst of exasperation, a new missionary once asked me, 'Why do Japanese people have to keep taking their shoes on and off all the time?'

As missionaries, we make it our aim to learn the language and culture of the country in which we minister. We need to make such adaptations, or we will ultimately put the brakes on our ministry. In the example above, you will not endear yourself to your Japanese hosts by tracking dirt in to their homes on the soles of your shoes! Your credibility will be lost, and so, for the time being at least, is your opportunity to share Jesus.

As we have welcomed new workers to the field, we have found that some immediately try to do all things Japanese. They sleep on the floor, they eat Japanese food and drink, and they watch Japanese cartoons (*anime*) on the Internet and so on. In many ways, this is good. We want missionaries to be enthusiastic about their new country and its culture. However, after a few months, the enthusiasm can begin to wane. What then?

How can we judge between those aspects of culture to which we must adapt for fear of compromising our witness, as opposed to those aspects of culture which don't need to apply to us personally? This is a much harder decision. For myself, I look washed out and ill in pastels, beige, grey and black. Do I need to dress in those colours to be truly adapted to my culture, or can I afford to wear brighter colours without standing out so much that the message of Jesus is overlooked? What about food, drink and lifestyle issues? Japanese people often sleep on the floor—do missionaries need to? Is it wrong to want to eat cheese or drink fresh milk—even if they aren't often available where you live? How do we decide where we need to adapt?

'Though I am free and belong to no one', says Paul, 'I have made myself a slave to everyone, to win as many as possible . . . I have become all things to all people so that by all possible means I might save some. I do all this for the sake of the gospel, that I may share in its blessings' (1 Corinthians 9:19, 22b–23).

First things first: God has given us freedom as believers. We are not to be a people bound by rules, although we recognise that God has given us clear instructions about how to live a life that pleases him. Second, however, notice that Paul says that he has made himself a slave to everyone to win as many as possible; he has become all things to all people so that by *all possible means* he might save some. What powerful statements! We too are called to follow in the footsteps of Jesus, who 'made himself nothing', and to take Paul as our mentor in giving up our freedoms.

I once heard a speaker comment on the difference between the proverb; 'When in Rome do as the Romans do' and these verses in 1 Corinthians 9. The difference is the *desire* that lies behind the words. The proverb about Rome is about our own comfort and convenience. Paul, however, was focused on the comfort and needs of those he was trying to reach. The speaker talked about the need to put ourselves in an uncomfortable position so that those we are trying to reach don't have to. What a helpful way of summarising the need for cultural adaptation!

The key is love. Paul was not a chameleon, but he showed love and gave up his freedom for the sake of the gospel. The same speaker said that we are not called to be jelly for the gospel. Neither should we be like concrete. We should be more like a feather duster which adapts its shape to the needs around us!

Interact

1   Make a list of what you enjoy and appreciate about your host culture and praise God for it.
2   Make a list of what you find more difficult in your new culture and talk to God about it.
3   Ask God to show you if you need to repent of any attitudes in regard to your host culture.
4   Ask God to show you new ways of learning to appreciate and adapt to your new culture.
5   Talk with a friend or older missionary about your struggles and listen to theirs. Pray together.
6   Ask God to help you to be true to the person he made you to be, but also to adapt in ways that are appropriate.

Prayer

Father thank you that you made me, me. Thank you that you determined the times set for me and the exact places where I should live so that those around me might reach out and find you. Wow! What a privilege to be part of your amazing plan. Lord, help me to find things I enjoy and appreciate about this culture and forgive me for knocking the people here or the way they do things sometimes. Lord, please help me to be true to the person you've made me, but also help me to show such love to those around me as to make myself their slave, for the sake of the gospel. Lord, that's hard, and I won't manage it alone. Please help me. Amen.

Culture Shock and Cultural Mistakes

om had been in Africa for six months and he was *hot*! He was sick of being hot. He missed the seasons; he wanted to wear a sweater! Why did this country have to be so hot all the time?

Louise was tired of living in a country that drove on the other side of the road. She had to cross the road differently; she had to drive differently. It was so annoying!

Megan's family in her home country didn't understand her feelings as a new missionary and that stressed her out. She knew they couldn't understand, but she was cross with them all the same.

Two other new missionaries used to ring each other regularly and say, "You know what, I hate ****!"** In their frustration and culture shock they criticised their host country. Culture shock isn't pretty.

What about all those bloopers we make when we try to talk? 'Have you got any *himitsu* (secrets)'? asked one missionary to a Japanese shop assistant. He wanted to ask, 'Have you got any *hachimitsu* (honey)?' No wonder the shop assistant looked taken aback! Of course, cultural mistakes aren't limited to language. How many new workers to Africa have attempted to receive a gift with their left hand—when that hand is reserved for personal hygiene? How many people have paid over the odds in the market because they couldn't bargain properly?

Living and working in a new culture is hard work. It can be merely embarrassing, or downright humiliating, or annoying or really depressing. What does God's word say that can help us as we get to grips with culture, and with the inevitable culture shock and cultural mistakes that follow?

> 'Whatever happens, conduct yourselves in a manner worthy of the gospel of Christ . . .' (Philippians 1:27a).

'Conduct yourselves in a manner worthy of the gospel of Christ'

The Philippian Christians were facing strong persecution, but Paul calls on them to conduct themselves in a manner worthy of the gospel of Christ. Wherever we live, people are watching us. But, if we live in another culture—and especially if we don't blend in easily—people watch us even more. Do our actions and reactions show that we love Jesus? We have a heavy responsibility both as Christians, and even more especially as missionaries, to live in a way that honours Jesus.

'Whatever happens . . .'

What has happened to you recently? Have you been embarrassed or humiliated because you blew it in your language learning? Perhaps you are simply fed up with the system, or maybe you lost your temper with someone recently. The phrase 'Whatever happens . . .' in this verse is a constant challenge to any Christian. We can all act in a manner worthy of the gospel when things are going well, but it's much harder when you make a mistake or are experiencing culture shock.

> Therefore if you have any encouragement from being united with Christ, if any comfort from his love, if any common sharing in the Spirit, if any tenderness and compassion, then make my joy complete by being like-minded, having the same love, being one in spirit and of one mind. Do nothing out of selfish ambition or vain conceit. Rather, in humility value others above yourselves. (Philippians 2:1–3).

Paul, writing from prison no less, knows from personal experience just how hard it is to react in a manner worthy of the gospel. But look at the words he uses in the passage above: encouragement, comfort, fellowship, tenderness and compassion. All these wonderful things belong to the Philippian Christians because they are united with Jesus. Therefore, having received all this, he calls them to show love, to be united in spirit and purpose and to be humble. We too have received all these things because we are united to Jesus. We too, therefore, are called to show love, unity and humility. As you face another cultural mistake, ask Jesus to fill you with humility. As you fight with feelings of anger about an aspect of culture that is driving you round the bend, ask God to give you a special portion of his love.

One year, my home church chose Philippians 1:27a as its motto text. The pastor concluded his sermon on the text with just three words: *Whatever, Walk, Worthy*!

Interact

1 Meditate on Philippians 1 and 2.
2 List your recent cultural mistakes—how can you avoid similar bloopers next time?
3 Is there some study, or someone you could talk with, to help you consider these issues?
4 'It's not wrong, it's just different.' Do you agree? How could this apply in your situation?
5 List what you are struggling with in your culture. Commit it all in to God's hands.
6 Confess your sin of a critical attitude if necessary. Ask God to give you his love for what you find difficult. Do you need to ask forgiveness of someone?
7 Living in a new culture is hard work. Do you need to take time out to rest or to have fun?

Prayer

Lord Jesus, I confess before you my sins of pride, anger, a lack of love and over-control. Please forgive me and give me your power to change. Thank you that you died to wash away my sin. Help me to take control of my negative thoughts and to bring them before your throne, as I remember your forgiveness and love for me. Please help me always to walk in a manner worthy of Jesus. In his name I pray, amen.

Emotional
Challenges

Home?

*B*eing brought up in Congo, Central Africa until the age of five had its advantages. I was free to roam all over, watched out for by various aunties and uncles. I climbed trees — and fell out of them! I ate freshly roasted peanuts, corn on the cob, grapefruits and bananas by the dozen. With my family I walked across rickety rope bridges, with only wood slats for my feet, and quite a few of those were missing. I came across exotic and not-so-friendly creatures, like the giant ants under our swing. But Congo was not my home. Congolese kids made fun of me for my white skin. I was left out of games. I didn't understand what the other kids said or the games they played. I wasn't included. I didn't fit.

To my surprise, when we returned to the UK as a family, the British kids laughed at me, too. They thought I'd be black. I didn't know their games. I didn't have a TV, and I didn't know how to play at being a 'Charlie's Angel' — I'd never even seen the TV show. I didn't like the food they ate. I wasn't included. I didn't fit. The UK was not my home.

I struggled for years to understand my place in the world. Was I Congolese? I didn't look it. I didn't speak French. Was I British? I might look it, but I didn't feel it. I seemed to feel different than how my friends felt. Who was I, and where was my home?

At the age of twenty-one, I returned to the tiny place, off-the-beaten-track, where I was born: Kimpese, which translated means, 'the place of the cockroach.' It's not on many world maps — it's too small — but it's important to me because it's where I began life.

But when I got there, I was hot. I was tired and overwhelmed. I was panicky. I stayed in a house by myself with a house helper caring for my laundry and food. Like the cake he made me—because I had a hankering for cake—and which he left under a fly screen. Only when I cut in to it, it collapsed having been totally consumed by ants except the very surface shell. None left for me! It seemed to summarise my feelings of not belonging in Congo—it felt like I was falling apart. I cried many tears about a place to belong. I surely didn't belong in Congo, but then neither did I belong in the UK. It all added up to feelings of rootlessness, a lack of clear direction in life and unhappiness.

The change happened when I attended a meeting of the Christian doctors' and nurses' fellowship. Like many African meetings, it was *very* long, and it was hot and sticky. It was also in French, which I spoke, but after quite a long message, my mind began to drift to the children I could see running around through the open walls. Oh to be free like them!

Suddenly the speaker said the most surprising phrase: 'Is God calling you to leave Congo behind?' Now I was definitely *not* listening by that point, but somehow the Holy Spirit grabbed my wandering attention and allowed me to hear that question. My answer was absolutely unequivocal. The answer was 'Yes'. I knew beyond doubt in that moment that God was calling me to leave Congo behind. I was free of the need to be there, to live there and to serve there. I received prayer and was set free to live and serve elsewhere.

That summer this verse from Hebrews became my life's theme; 'For here we do not have an enduring city, but we are looking for the city that is to come' (Hebrews 13:14).

I don't feel at home in Congo—I am not Congolese. I don't feel at home in the UK, even though my passport says I'm British. I have worked in Senegal in West Africa, but I don't feel at home there, either. I have now worked in Japan for eighteen years on and off, but I don't feel at home there, either. But you know what, it doesn't matter anymore. Heaven is my home. I am waiting for that enduring city. I'm looking forward to it. One day I will be completely, finally at home. In the meantime, I am called to be at home wherever I am because that is where God has called me to be.

It isn't always easy. I still long to fit sometimes. I long to be able to have a home of my own and settle in the UK. I long to fit in to Japanese culture instead of standing out as a foreigner—no matter how good my linguistic and cultural skills ever get to be. But the restlessness has gone. I can live at peace. I am at home where God has placed me now, and I will be finally and fully at home when he takes me to his eternal home in heaven.

Interact

1 Have you ever felt homeless or rootless? How did it feel?
2 Do you need to forgive anyone who helped exacerbate those feelings of homelessness?
3 Is it appropriate to share your feelings with someone? If so, with whom?
4 What can you do practically in your current situation to help yourself feel more at home?
5 Write a poem or a prayer to express your feelings and your thanks to God for his provision of an eternal home.

Prayer

Thank you, Lord, that you made me for yourself: you gave me the life I have. You made me special. Thank you, too, that you made me for heaven. On days when I don't fit in with my friends, my colleagues, my family or those I seek to serve, help me to remember that wherever you place me, I can be at home because you are there. It is the very best place for me to be. Thank you so much that ultimately I will know the perfect rest of my heavenly home. Please help me to remember and know this comfort on the days when I feel homeless, homesick and rootless. In the powerful name of Jesus, Amen.

Homesick

*C*heese, sausages, green fields and countryside, mountains, hearing your own language in the street, your friends, your family—what are the things you miss from home? When we first become missionaries, the excitement of our adopted country generally fills our minds and hearts. However, after a little while—and the timing is different for everyone—cravings for the things we know and love, as well as the people we know and love, sweep over us once in a while. For me, I miss being able to go to a supermarket in the UK and find so much food that I love to eat! (I am a particularly fussy individual.) I miss being able to wander around and blend in. I stick out like the proverbial sore thumb, and I don't like that. I often wish I might go home just for the weekend. I have a job to do, and I want to do it, but I do miss everyone. Homesickness is very real.

> For we do not have a high priest who is unable to feel sympathy for our weaknesses, but we have one who has been tempted in every way, just as we are—yet he did not sin. Let us then approach God's throne of grace with confidence, so that we may receive mercy and find grace to help us in our time of need. (Hebrews 4:15–16)

These verses have encouraged me time and time again—not just in relation to my tendency toward sin, but in the many struggles and challenges which come in life. 'For we do not have a high priest who is unable to feel sympathy for our weaknesses . . .' I have many weaknesses, just like you. One of those weaknesses is that I get homesick sometimes. But the absolutely fantastic and truly amazing good news is that Jesus understands. He *is* able to sympathise with this weakness. Just think, Jesus left heaven; he left his father—and he came here, to this world so full of sin, disease and evil. Was Jesus homesick? I don't think we can say that exactly, but surely he had a longing for heaven and for his father.

When I had been a missionary in Japan for six months, I wrote the following poem. It's not all about homesickness, but I think homesickness shines all the way through it.

Lord Jesus, if you can feel sympathy for my weaknesses,
then you know how I feel today.
Were you ever tempted to be jealous, Lord? What about?
The people around you who lived 'normal' human lives?
People who had their family always around them?
People who fell in love and got married?
People who had a permanent home, with comfortable beds
to sleep in?
Did you long to be like other people?
Did you long to change places sometimes?
If you did, then you'll know how I feel today.
How jealous I am of other people's lives; of those who
have family always around them; of those with a permanent address.
How I long to be like other people; how I long to change
places sometimes.
Lord, I feel like that today. Please help me.
I can't help myself—I've tried.
Only you can help me, because you alone can sympathise
with my weaknesses—but you have overcome them.

On one occasion, when we were saying 'goodbye' to some missionary friends from the UK who were going to work in Pakistan, I said, 'But we won't see you for years!' She replied, saying something like, 'Let's not be sad about the time we won't have together, but let's treasure the time we have had'. What wise advice!

Susan Miller of *Focus on the Family* says that we need to *cherish* those things, places and people that we love. However, we must *cling* to God and him alone. (4) So often in our lives, we get it the wrong way around. We end up *clinging* to the things, places and people we love. When we do that, we experience more grief than we are made to do. We must learn to *cherish* the things that change and *cling* to the things that don't.

Interact

1   Thank God for all the good things, people and places in your life.
2   Perhaps you might like to write to some of the people who came to mind and thank them for their love and friendship.
3   You might like to make a collage of people or places or things that God has given to remind you to be thankful.
4   Ask God to help you *cherish* all the wonderful gifts he has given you.
5   Ask God's forgiveness if you need to, for *clinging* to the wrong things.
6   Thank Jesus that he knows your weaknesses and has overcome them.
7   Ask Jesus to give you mercy and grace in your homesickness.
8   Plan some practical steps to learn to enjoy the place and the people where God has placed you.

Prayer

It is a thing most wonderful,
almost too wonderful to be,
that God's own Son should come from heaven,
and die to save a child like me.

I cannot tell how he would love
a child so weak and full of sin;

his love must be most wonderful,
if he could die my love to win.

—William Walsham How (1823–1897)

Amen.

Self-Worth

I remember well the day I received the result of my public language exam — I'd failed. In fact, I'd done hardly any better than the last time I took it the year before! Dejection. Humiliation. Hopeless. Worthless. Give it up. Go home. All these thoughts and feelings rose to the surface, like scum on a cooking pot.

I realised later that I wasn't just upset because I had failed the exam. I was upset because I was giving the result of that exam too much power over me. Instead of the exam simply being a measure of my language ability, I saw it as a measure of my worth as a missionary, as well as my worth as a human being. No wonder I was so unreasonably distressed. I wrote in my journal that day, 'It's not that *I'm* not good enough, but that *my Japanese* is not good enough'.

What makes you doubt your worth as a human being or as a missionary? Some of us lug very heavy suitcases with us as we journey through life — suitcases stuffed with failed relationships, a difficult family life, bullying as a child or being the geeky one who wasn't good at sports. What is it for you? Perhaps in your current situation, you have fallen in to the trap of comparison with other missionaries. Maybe their language ability is better than yours, perhaps their Bible translation is streaks ahead of yours, perhaps their church is baptising more people than yours or perhaps their family seem so godly — compared to yours! What is it that makes you doubt your worth?

Isaiah 41:8–10 gives us encouragement and certainty in our calling and God's enabling;

> But you, O Israel, my servant, Jacob, whom I have
> chosen, you descendants of Abraham my friend, I
> took you from the ends of the earth, from its farthest
> corners I called you. I said, 'You are my servant'; I
> have chosen you and have not rejected you. So do not
> fear, for I am with you; do not be dismayed, for I am
> your God. I will strengthen you and help you; I will
> uphold you with my righteous right hand.

Try re-reading the passage above, putting your name in place of
Israel and Jacob.

As Christians, as missionaries, we are God's servants. God has
chosen you and me. Choosing is a deliberate action, not accidental.
We didn't slip in through the back door. No, we have been chosen, as
the modern descendants of Abraham, who was called God's friend.
John 15:14 says of us; 'You are my friends if you do what I command'. What a privilege.

Isaiah 41:9 says that we have been taken from the ends of the earth,
called by God from its farthest corners. You can almost picture God
moving to and fro across the world, hunting high and low, around
bends and in dark corners for his people. Luke 19:10 tells us, 'For
the Son of Man came to seek and to save the lost'. We are the people
he came looking for. Just let that sink in for a moment. God came
looking for you.

God has searched for us. God has chosen us. Verse 9 also tells
us that God has not rejected us. We may have been bullied at school
or had parents who ignored us or mistreated us. We may have issues
with language learning or we might be struggling with our work, *but*
God has not rejected us. Jesus says to his disciples, 'In this world you
will have trouble. But take heart! I have overcome the world' (John
16:33b). God has not rejected us—praise him!

Isaiah 41:10 shows us the practical result of God's seeking,
choosing and acceptance of us. We have no need to be afraid. God
is with us. As Jesus tells his disciples at the end of Matthew, 'And
surely I am with you always, to the very end of the age' (Matthew
28:20b). What comfort; what assurance. We don't need to be dis-
mayed because the God of the Bible is our God, and he has sought

us out, gathered us from around the world, chosen us specially and he is with us. What have we to worry about?

Not only do we gain a right sense of self and our worth before the God of the universe, he promises in these verses to strengthen, help and uphold us. God's strength is so much greater than our own feeble little muscles! We need God's help because we can't do it alone. He promises to uphold us—what a wonderful and releasing thought.

We live in a dark and fallen world, which constantly tells us of our lack of self-worth, our sin and our failure. God tells us the truth. 'So don't be afraid; you are worth more than many sparrows' (Matthew 10:31).

Interact

1   In what ways are you struggling with self-worth? Alternatively, do you recognise a prideful attitude in your heart? Talk to God about these things and confess your unbelief and pride.
2   Is there a particular situation that is causing you to struggle at the moment? Take time now to pray about it.
3   Write out Isaiah 41:8–10 with your name in it. Do some art-work or make a poster to remind you of the truth of these words for you.
4   Meditate on the verse; 'So don't be afraid; you are worth more than many sparrows' (Matthew 10:31).
5   Praise God for his love, his choosing, his calling, his enabling and his presence.

Prayer

Thank you, God, that you loved me so much that you sent Jesus in to this world to die for my sins so that I might become your child. Thank you that you deemed me so valuable that you entered this dark and fallen world and found me. Please forgive me when I doubt my worth and value before you. Please forgive me when I look to other people and other things to give me self-worth. Thank you that you promise to be with me and to enable me. Help me always to look to you for my ultimate value and worth. In Jesus' name, amen.

Unappreciated

'scrubbed out the first toilet and started on the second. A candidate entered the first with muddy shoes. The floor was still wet. When she left, I returned and did the first again . . . This continued for some little time with a rising sense of frustration . . .' writes Helen Roseveare, missionary to the Congo in 1950s and '60s in her book *Give me this mountain*. (5) Helen's supervisor then asked her 'For whom are you scrubbing this floor?' 'For you, of course; you sent me here', replied Helen. 'I've never forgotten her answer', continues Helen. 'No my dear. If you are doing it for me, you may as well go home. You'll never satisfy me. You're doing it for the Lord, and *He* saw the first time you cleaned it. That is now tomorrow's dirt.'

These words resonate with me! Caring for new workers and running a language school has parts that no one sees, except my husband, me and God. I can spend hours writing timetables, or setting up apartments, or talking with people, or tidying up. My husband might spend his day fixing toilets, or mending chairs, or filling in forms in Japanese, or preparing orientation classes. Very often what we do is unseen, but I'm glad to say largely appreciated. Sometimes though, it can feel like an unending struggle to keep the ship afloat, and nobody seems to notice or care.

Do you sometimes feel unappreciated? Do you feel that your family or your church or your supporters simply don't understand what you do? I'm sure you must have similar moments of frustration. You wouldn't be human otherwise. Helen Roseveare's supervisor's words are incredibly apt for such situations and frustrations.

'If you are doing it for me, you may as well go home. You'll never satisfy me'. We usually start off working for the Lord. We became missionaries because we felt God's call on our lives. We may begin each day talking with and listening to God, but sometimes along the way, we start working—not for God, but for ourselves or other people. This will never bring us satisfaction! We might as well give up. Colossians 3:17 tells us, 'And whatever you do, whether in word or deed, do it all in the name of the Lord Jesus, giving thanks to God the Father through him'.

Whether it's cleaning toilets, fixing chairs, making timetables, changing nappies or diapers, memorising vocabulary, picking up after others, preaching, sharing our faith, all must be done—word and deed—in the name of the Lord Jesus and for his glory on earth.

'You're doing it for the Lord, and He saw the first time you cleaned it'. What we do may go unnoticed and unappreciated by those around us, but we are doing it for God, and he knows what we have done in our service in his name. When Sarah's servant Hagar had been cruelly mistreated and cast out and was alone, she gave God the name, '. . . the God who sees me' (Genesis 16:13). Even if no one else appreciates or sees our service in his name, God does. What a wonderful comfort and encouragement to keep on in our service of him.

'That is now tomorrow's dirt.' Among missionaries, there can be an unhelpful tendency toward perfectionism. Of course, we must all strive to serve God in whatever way we can to the very best of our ability and according to his work within us, but sometimes we don't know when to quit! Perfectionism can take over, and our pride comes to the fore. When we have done the work allocated to today, we can stop and deal with tomorrow's work, *tomorrow*. Matthew 6:34 tells us, 'Therefore do not worry about tomorrow, for tomorrow will worry about itself. Each day has enough trouble of its own'.

Interact

1 What work are you involved in which you feel no one notices or appreciates? Make a list.
2 Take your list before your Heavenly Father who is the 'God who sees'. Tell him about it.

3   Receive from him his 'well-done' and ask for his forgiveness for focusing on the admiration of those around you, rather than his.
4   Forgive those around you who may not appreciate your work.
5   Ask for God's supernatural help to work for him and not for those around you—whatever you do.
6   Ask God to help you know when to quit. Ask for his forgiveness for any tendency toward perfectionism or self-reliance.
7   Receive his peace as you continue to serve him, and him alone, faithfully.

Prayer

O God my Father, who sees all I do, thank you. Thank you that you have saved me, that you have called me and that you see and appreciate my service of you. Forgive me when I focus on working for other people, rather than for you. Help me to live and work each day for your glory—not my own and not other people's. Help me, too, to leave tomorrow in your hands and not to grab it with my own. In Jesus' name and for his glory, amen.

It's All Too Much!

*E*lijah bursts on to the scene in 1 Kings 17 and so begins a period of closeness with God, prophecy and miracles. In the power of the spirit of God, Elijah predicts the weather, is fed by ravens, is the means of life-sustaining food for a widow and raises the dead—all in just in one chapter! He continues on to confront King Ahab, calls down fire from heaven, prays for rain and runs faster than any Olympian. In just over three years, Elijah has a dramatic and successful ministry.

But then, along comes Jezebel who says, 'May the gods deal with me, be it ever so severely, if by this time tomorrow I do not make your life like that of one of them' (that is, like the prophets of Baal who have all been killed; 1 Kings 19:2). God's man of the moment— successful Elijah—is terrified and runs for his *life*. How things can change, even in an instant. We join him as he sits under a tree and cries out to God, 'I have had enough, LORD', he said. 'Take my life; I am no better than my ancestors' (1 Kings 19:4).

Have you ever felt and prayed like Elijah did at that point? 'I've had enough, Lord, please take my life'. My guess is yes, and perhaps you even feel like this at the moment. As I shared earlier in this book, in my first year as a missionary, I prayed similarly to this more times than I can tell you. Elijah is in just such a place in this chapter.

One missionary shared his desire to run on a particularly disastrous Sunday morning, trying to deal with his children, sort out the church and the people in it and preach a sermon in another language! He wondered to himself, 'What am I doing here? Why don't I just stomp out the door and never come back? I turned to (my wife) and mouthed the words, "I can't go up there and preach!" She mouthed back, "You have to." With no apparent chance of escape I bowed my head in the thirty seconds left to me and prayed for help.' Perhaps you have witnessed to someone more times than you can count, but they still refuse to listen. Perhaps you feel your ministry has achieved nothing. If that's the way you feel or perhaps the way someone you know feels, you aren't the first.

But look what happens next to Elijah. Elijah is asleep in the desert all alone, without a soul for company—just his tortured thoughts, his fear and stress. But God does not leave him like that! He sends his angel to Elijah to bring him life-sustaining food and drink, not just once, but twice. Not only that, the angel got a fire going, which no doubt brought Elijah warmth and comfort; it gets pretty cold in the desert at night. God knew *exactly* where his servant was and what he needed. And God met those needs—of warmth, comfort, food, drink, encouragement and company. Perhaps you could even say that God met Elijah's need for rest and sleep. I don't find it easy to sleep when my mind is disturbed. Perhaps part of God's meeting of Elijah's needs was in granting him sleep in the first place. Please, be encouraged: cry out to God like Elijah. He knows where you are, what you struggle with and how best to meet your need. Allow him to minister to you—perhaps through others, perhaps even through angels.

Once Elijah was physically strengthened, he met with God at Horeb. So begins restoration part two, this time meeting Elijah's spiritual needs and recommissioning him for the task ahead. First Kings 19:9b says, 'What are you doing here, Elijah?' asked God. God graciously gives Elijah the opportunity to explain his problem—as if God didn't know! So Elijah responds, 'I have been very zealous for the LORD God Almighty. The Israelites have rejected your covenant, torn down your altars, and put your prophets to death with the sword. I am the only one left, and now they are trying to kill me too' (1 Kings 19:10). Elijah expresses his frustrations to God. He's done everything right, but . . . Have you ever said something like, 'But God, I've willingly done everything you've asked, but people aren't listening, it isn't making any difference and now look at the state I'm in?' God wants to hear from you; he wants to hear your frustrations and your fears. Talk to him like Elijah did.

God then graciously and magnificently reveals himself to Elijah but not in the tornado-like wind, not in the trembling earthquake and not in the raging fire. 'After the fire came a gentle whisper . . .' (1 Kings 19:12). That gentle whisper or 'still small voice' was the very presence of God in that place.

I am left wondering why God didn't show himself in the wind, the earthquake and the fire. After all, he clearly caused them all, and he could have shown himself through them. Perhaps it's because Elijah has seen God stop rain and bring rain. He has seen God raise people to life. He has seen God's fire. Elijah has seen the dramatic stuff. Dramatics isn't what Elijah needs at this point. I think God chooses meets with Elijah in the most gentle and personal way possible—God knows he needs the personal touch.

In this whole situation, Elijah's perspective has been skewed. Elijah has just seen God work mightily and yet he doesn't trust God for his own situation—desperate though it is. He has ignored the existence of the faithful believer Obadiah we read about in chapter 18, not to mention all the other prophets hiding in caves. In reality, Elijah shouldn't have been at Horeb, but God being the gracious God he is, met Elijah there. Not only that, he met him with gentleness and a re-calling to do his work. First Kings 19:15 says, 'The LORD said to him, "Go back the way you came . . ."'

We too sometimes find ourselves feeling like Elijah and sometimes that's because we also have our perspective wrong, but not always. Whatever the case, believe that God knows and cares for you and wants to minister to you—just like he did to Elijah.

Interact

1   Meditate on 1 Kings 17–19 and make a note of points of similarity and difference between Elijah and yourself.

2   Read C. S. Lewis' *The Horse and His Boy* (6), especially chapter 11, 'The Unwelcome Traveller'.

3   Meditate on Psalms 4, 6 or 7, or other Psalms of lament. Write your own Psalm to God based on these and your own experiences and feelings.

4   Confess your lack of trust and skewed perspective to God and seek his forgiveness if you need to.

5   Read John 21:15–17. Thank God for his care for Elijah, for Peter and for you—for his physical care, his spiritual care and his complete restoration.

6   If you need to, consider talking to a trusted friend, pastor or fellow missionary. Don't suffer and struggle alone with feelings of fear, depression or failure.

7   Consider whether you need to take some time off for holiday or spiritual renewal. Talk to someone about that possibility if that is appropriate.

Prayer

Thank you, Lord, that you met Elijah at his point of need. Thank you that you didn't leave him alone. Thank you that you gave him physical and spiritual refreshment. Lord, please meet me at my point of need. Sometimes I don't even know what I need or what is best for me. Lord, in those times, help me to trust in you and in your gentle love for me. In Jesus' name, amen.

Organisational
Challenges

Mission Culture

'*If* you want to go fast, go alone. If you want to go far, go together'. So says an African proverb.

Many of us working overseas or in culturally different situations have joined a mission to enable and help us in our ministry. Some of us work in parts of the world where even just beginning to work without language, culture or a knowledge of how the system works, would make it extraordinarily difficult, if not impossible, to work independently. Hence the role of a mission—to help us to go far in mission together.

But as I am sure you are aware, a mission is not a mission, is not a mission! Every organisation has a unique set of beliefs, values, practices and goals. Of course, there is significant overlap in some areas between organisations, but the 'feel' of different missions—even those working within the same country—is very different. The question a new missionary needs to ask themselves is "How well do I know, understand and appreciate my particular mission's culture?" Because, believe you me, it does have one!

In our role as those who welcomed new workers to the field, this is an area which often caught new mission partners unawares. Most new workers prepare themselves well for the practical and emotional changes ahead as they enter a new country and culture. They understand that they will need to learn new ways of doing things, new ways of relating and new ways of speaking. What they don't always expect is that they will also need to get to know the culture of the organisation they have joined.

So, what about you—how much do you know? How does your organisation manage its finances? How does it make decisions? How often do you meet altogether? How does your organisation set its overall goals? How is time off for holiday, compassionate leave, sick leave and so forth dealt with? Does your organisation simply encompass a group of independent workers—like a whole bunch of people driving self-drive camper vans or SUVs? Or does it act more like a fellowship or community of believers, like travellers together on a long-distance bus? Do you know? And do you know why they do what they do, in the way that they do it? Of course, you may have done some research about some of these areas before you joined your organisation—I hope you did—but now that you're a part of it, there is more to learn!

As new missionaries, you will need to take the time to get to know how your organisation works and to get to know the people in it—particularly perhaps if it is more of the 'long-distance bus' sort of mission, as opposed to the 'self-drive camper van or SUV' type of mission.

A few pointers as you do that . . .

Galatians 6:10 says, 'Therefore, as we have opportunity, let us do good to all people, especially to those who belong to the family of believers'. Let me encourage you to do good to the family of believers who make up your mission! Your mission needs you: you need them. Many missions can act as a tremendous support for their members, becoming even closer than family in some instances. Get to know people—eat together, share together, pray together. Seek how you can do good to your fellow missionaries. You probably joined your mission for what it could offer you. That's OK, but consider what you can offer in return and how you can serve them.

Ephesians 5:21 says, 'Submit to one another out of reverence for Christ'. Being part of a mission also means that we need to be considerate of others and their feelings above our own. We also need to hold disputable opinions lightly.

Hebrews 13:17 tells us, 'Have confidence in your leaders and submit to their authority, because they keep watch over you as those who must give an account. Do this so that their work will be a joy, not a burden, for that would be of no benefit to you'. You have joined an organisation and while it may not meet all your needs and you may not agree with every aspect of its operation, you need to obey this passage of the Bible. Especially at the beginning when you may not know quite so much about the way your organisation works, it can be easy to be critical and defensive. You will need to ask God for his help on this one.

Last, Colossians 3:13 commands us, 'Bear with each other and forgive one another if any of you has a grievance against someone. Forgive as the Lord forgave you'. In any mission situation, there are going to be upsets and misunderstandings, and sometimes, sadly, deep disputes. Many missionaries leave their fields of service for just this sort of reason. We must be those who bear with one another and who forgive *any* grievances we may have. It is hard, but it must be done, or else we bring the gospel itself in to disrepute.

Interact

1   What are your mission's values — its true values, not the ones it says it has?
2   What is your mission's culture?
3   What can you do practically to get to know your mission and the other missionaries? Come up with two or three practical steps to help you in this.
4   How can you do good to those in your mission?
5   In what areas might you need to submit to others?
6   How are you getting on at obeying your leaders? Do you need to repent of unhelpful attitudes or behaviour?
7   Do you need to ask someone's forgiveness, or do you need to forgive someone else?

Prayer

Lord, thank you so much that there are mission organisations that can help me do what I believe you've called me to do. I name before you now the leaders of my organisation and ask that you would strengthen, bless and use them in your name. Lord, please help me to get to know others and do good to them. Lord, you know I struggle with submission, both in terms of authority and to those around me who think differently from me. Please help me to look at Jesus when I am tempted to stand my ground or answer back. Lord, forgive me for when I rebel and displease you. In Jesus' name and for his sake, amen.

Time and Accountability

A newcomer to Japan was put on a train by the missionary he had been visiting, in order to visit another area of the country. He nervously asked, 'But how will I know when to get off the train since I can't read?' 'Simple', the missionary replied, 'Just get off the train at 2.47pm and you'll be there!'

As you read this, I wonder where you are in the world. Are you in the Democratic Republic of the Congo, where time has an 'elastic' quality? Are you in Switzerland, famous for clocks? Are you in Japan where everything runs like clockwork? Or are you in Spain, where *mañana* is the phrase and attitude of choice? Whatever, whenever— our world cultures have many different attitudes toward time. For those of us who work in a culture different to our own, there are often adjustments to be made in how we view time and how we use time. Not only that, but if you belong to a mission organisation, you may well find that they also have different values in this area, and you may need to learn to adapt and flex. It isn't easy in either situation.

We may experience not only cultural struggles with time, but we may have personal struggles, too. As individuals, we have been brought up in different countries, different home environments and have different personalities—all of which affect how we view time and how we use time. 'Procrastination is the thief of time'. 'A race against the clock'. 'In the nick of time'. These well-known phrases may describe some of our feelings about time. It often feels as though we have too little time to do all that must be done, and sometimes even when we *do* have time, we waste it.

In contrast, the Bible says, 'Before the mountains were born or you brought forth the whole world, from everlasting to everlasting you are God . . .' (Psalm 90:2). God is eternal; outside time. However, Ecclesiastes 3:1 says of us and our lives, 'There is a time for everything, and a season for every activity under the heavens'. While Mordecai in the book of Esther reminds her (and us), 'And who knows but that you have come to your royal position for such a time as this?' (Esther 4:14b). God ordains time and circumstances in order that we might be used for his purposes and to show his glory.

So how do you use your time? How well do you manage your time? Does one of the phrases above describe your battle with time? Or do you have a sense of being in the right place at the right time in God's amazing plan?

Many mission partners are free to structure their days as they wish. Of course, they will have certain responsibilities; for example; getting the kids to school or home schooling, preparing a Bible study or a sermon, getting the housework done, visiting someone at home or in hospital, language study, translating the Bible, getting in touch with supporters at home and a myriad of other things, too. They will also need to make time for personal Bible study and prayer. However, unless a mission partner works in a school, college, office or other structured work environment, they are often free to direct and plan their days as seems best. This is both a tremendous blessing and occasionally a burden!

On the plus side, it gives great flexibility. It may mean couples can share childcare and housework. It can mean that one can plan for especially busy days to be followed by quieter days. It can mean that working in the evening allows you to take a walk in the afternoon to enjoy the world God has made. However, with this *flexibility* comes with significant *responsibility*. How do you ensure that you put in a good day's work? Are you actually working hard enough? Are you giving value for money to your supporters, and before the Lord? How much time have you spent on the Internet—browsing and chatting? How much time do you spend watching TV or DVDs? What is *your* favourite waste of time? On the other hand, are you working far too hard? How often do you enjoy personal time? How often are you home to pray with your kids before bedtime? When did you last take a holiday? Are you taking time to connect with those who love you? Are you taking time to wind down at the end of the day?

We worship and serve an eternal God, but we live in a time-bound world. That is always going to be a tension for as long as we live on this earth. We all have things we need to think through regarding our use of time, but perhaps Ephesians 5:15–16 should set our thinking in context; 'Be very careful, then, how you live—not as unwise but as wise, making the most of every opportunity, because the days are evil'.

Interact

1   Think through your home culture's attitude to time, your family's attitude to time and your personal attitude to time. Are you content with what you discover? If not, which aspects would you like to change? Ask God to help you in this area.

2   Think through your adopted country's attitude to time and—if you belong to a mission—think through your mission's attitude to time. What do you discover? Do you find this easy or difficult? Ask for God's grace as you live and work in your current situation.

3   Consider how well you manage your time. Do you plan carefully and get done what needs to be done? Or do you procrastinate and wait until the last minute? How is your current attitude and behaviour working? Do you want to change it? Ask God to help you do so.

4   Do you need to plan your activities more—if so, how are you going to do that?

5   Do you need to take some time off? Make plans before the Lord to do that.

6   Pray through Ephesians 5:15–16 for yourself. How are you going to put this into practice?

Prayer

Lord, I praise you for being eternal—from everlasting to everlasting. That is such a comfort to me. Thank you that you are never late; you are never in a rush. You are always just on time—your time. Thank you so much. Lord, you know my background, my culture, where I live now and how I use my time. Lord, please guide me to use my time wisely, to make the most of every opportunity. Help me to make time for everything you want me to do and be, and use me in your eternal purposes, like you used Esther and many others. For your glory's sake, amen.

When the Mission 'Gets in My Face'!

*I*n our home countries, most of us worked in secular, salary-paying employment before becoming missionaries. We were faithful members of a local church. We were in regular contact with family, even if we didn't live close by. In our home countries, these parts of our lives may well have been separate entities—perhaps with a few tangled connections here or there. Work colleagues may not have known our family, and unless we lived and worked in the same local area, it is likely that work colleagues didn't know our church friends. Becoming a member of a missionary society turns a lot of this on its head.

Suddenly, instead of receiving a salary, we receive an allowance, and sometimes we receive that only if our support is adequate or the exchange rate is favourable. But the biggest change of all for many of us is the fact that all three parts of our lives—work, church and family—are now intimately connected. Particularly for those working in more traditional missionary contexts, our work colleagues—often fellow missionaries—know our families and we know theirs. We 'hang out' together. And—perhaps particularly for new missionaries who may struggle to make relationships in the national church due to a lack of language—very often our closest church friends are the same people that we work with and the people that have become our family! All three compartments in our lives have merged.

In a traditional mission, missionaries are very often fiercely bound together through their common work, their life in the mission

119

family and the spiritual fellowship they experience with other missionaries. This brings both joys and challenges!

Challenges

1   Goldfish bowl effect—When we live and work and worship in close proximity, it can feel like all the other missionaries know all our personal business. Often that's true. Some of us, particularly perhaps those more private individuals, struggle with this.
2   No escape—In our home countries, we can perhaps 'let our hair down' at home or relax in church, while at work we are on duty. In a traditional mission context, we are often with the same people for work, leisure and worship. If we are having a problem with our work colleague, it will often affect our free time and our spiritual walk as a community.
3   The mission rules—OK? Before becoming missionaries, we (well, hopefully God) directed our own lives—where we chose to live, who we chose to spend time with, what work we did and so forth. When we become members of a mission, it can feel (and sometimes indeed it is the case) that the mission leaders direct not just our work, but how we live the rest of our lives, too! There aren't many of us who wouldn't fight against that.

Joys

1   Worldwide church—As mission workers we have the privilege of fellowship with God's people from all over the world in a way that those in our home churches may not. We have a foretaste of heaven. Revelation 7:9a says, 'After this I looked, and there before me was a great multitude that no one could count, from every nation, tribe, people and language, standing before the throne and before the Lamb'.
2   Broad family—Most of us leave our earthly families behind when we travel overseas for extended periods of time. This is a true sadness. However, God in his mercy gives us another

family in our brothers and sisters, aunties and uncles, nephews and nieces and grandpas and grandmas in our mission agency or in the national church. 'God sets the lonely in families, he leads out the prisoners with singing . . .' (Psalm 68:6).

3   Deepened relationships—Because many mission partners experience so much together in a way that wouldn't normally happen in our home countries, we can develop deep and lasting relationships with one another. There is camaraderie between fellow mission workers that is a spiritual blessing. 'Do not forsake your friend or a friend of your family, and do not go to your relative's house when disaster strikes you—better a neighbour nearby than a relative far away' (Proverbs 27:10).

4   Genuine holy living—Because there is no escape, we are all the more aware of the need for genuine holy living. 'As iron sharpens iron, so one person sharpens another' (Proverbs 27:17). God has given us colleagues to help us become more genuine and more holy.

As you reflect on your own situation and mission agency—or lack of one—there may well be other challenges and other joys, but ask yourself today what special things God has for you in your situation.

Interact

1   In what ways do you feel the mission is 'in your face'? Talk to God about it and write it in your journal.

2   Are there those in the organisation that you need to apologise to, talk with or thank? Make a list and set aside time today or during this week to do that.

3   Have you opened your heart to the good things your mission agency or people in it can do for you and your family? Think through your response by journaling.

4   Ask God to help you appreciate the joy of belonging to and serving with this part of his worldwide church.

5   Ask God to help you appreciate the extra mission family he's given you, and ask him to help you to open yourself up to

their help, advice and friendship. Not only that, ask God for good relationships where you can also be 'family' to them.

6   Ask God to help you to receive his training through your mission family.

7   'Therefore, as we have opportunity, let us do good to all people, especially to those who belong to the family of believers' (Galatians 6:10). Ask yourself; to whom in the mission family can you do good today?

Prayer

Thank you, Lord, for the people you have put around me. Thank you that I am not all alone. Thank you for people who love and care for me and who are trying to take your work forward in this country. But, Lord, help me to love them and forgive them, while remembering that their motives are good! Help me, too, to open my heart to this my mission family, and make me a blessing to them, too. Amen.

Conflict!

*J*ill and Dave came from different backgrounds, had contrasting personalities and held some very different ideas. Dave was a practical 'doer,' while Jill had at least twenty new ideas before breakfast. Theirs was never going to be a relationship made in heaven!

Abby and Lisa were a similar age, new to their mission field and had a lot in common in many ways, but they had very different ideas about child-rearing. It led to tension and conflict between them.

Linda was a morning person, but Mark was a 'night bird.' How could they work together when Linda's brain switched off after 8.30 pm, and Mark was just beginning to come alive?

In any team or mission situation, conflict is pretty much inevitable to a greater or lesser extent. I don't say this to depress you. I say it to encourage you so that you may know that when you find yourself in a conflict situation, you are not necessarily behaving in a sinful or un-Christian way. You aren't the first, and you won't be the last! The key question is how you deal with such conflict.

'Bear with each other and forgive one another if any of you has a grievance against someone. Forgive as the Lord forgave you. And over all these virtues put on love, which binds them all together in perfect unity' (Colossians 3:13–14). Believe me when I say that if you have joined a mission organisation, you will have plenty of opportunities to put the commands in this verse into practice! So let's take a look at them.

First, we are called to bear with each other. What does that mean? I think it means that there is no running away from a conflict situation.

It means that we need to press on through the conflict to try to find resolution, by God's grace. When we are in our home country, in a conflict situation there is a temptation simply to leave. If I don't like what's going on at my church, I can go to a different one! Similarly, if my work situation is tough, I am free to look for another job. However, in a mission situation, that option is often removed. That is no doubt a good thing, though admittedly a very hard thing. We have made a commitment to a mission or a church or a job, and there aren't many — or even any — alternatives. We are forced to press on through, to bear with one another and we surely need God's supernatural grace to do that. (Very occasionally, however, there may be times when people simply don't work well together — like Paul and Barnabas — or when the situation has reached a stalemate. However, I suspect these occasions are rarer than we might like to think.)

Second, this verse says that we are to forgive any grievances we may have against one another. I am challenged by this yet again. This verse doesn't say that we should forgive *some* grievances, but *any* grievances. That is to say, *all* grievances. Oh dear! Just this week, I have been upset by another missionary's ungrateful behaviour, yet another missionary's bad temper, yet another missionary's know-it-all attitude, and yet another missionary's failure to listen and understand. However, I am called, yes even commanded, to 'forgive *any* grievances' I have against my brothers and sisters! May God help me to be obedient.

Third, I am called to do this because I have already been forgiven by God. God, in Christ, has forgiven *my* bad behaviour, *my* bad temper, *my* superior attitude and *my* failure to listen. I am therefore expected to extend this godly forgiveness to my fellow mission workers. May God help me to know the depth of my own forgiveness in order that I might extend that to others.

Finally, Paul calls the Colossian Christians to 'put on love.' In Japanese, these verses read; 'put on love as a binding *obi*'. An *obi* is the wide belt or cummerbund worn around the waist with a kimono. On average, an *obi* is about four metres in length and wound around several times in various intricate designs. Our love as Christians must be equally as long — or even longer.

Interact

1 Who or what is upsetting you right now? Write in your journal about your feelings toward this person and about the situation.
2 Ask God to show you if you have sinned in your thoughts or dealings with this individual or in your handling of the situation. Confess those sins to God.
3 Praise God through prayer, writing or song for his forgiveness of your sins.
4 Make a definite act of forgiveness toward those who have hurt you. Perhaps you could write a prayer of forgiveness and commend the individual or situation to God.
5 Think through whether you need to make a time to discuss this relationship or conflict situation with someone you trust or someone in authority. Make a time to do that if appropriate.
6 Take a look at the Appendix (final page) *Dealing Positively with People I Find Difficult*

Prayer

Lord God, thank you that you have forgiven me all my sins. Help me to recognise the depths of my own depravity and the heights of your wonderful forgiveness. Help me to bear with my brothers and sisters for the sake of your gospel and your glory. Give me grace and strength beyond my own. Help me to forgive *whatever* grievances I have against your people and help me work toward a creative, loving solution. Amen.

Family
Challenges

Family—on the Field

'At first I coped fairly well, but then there came a time when the slightest thing would set me off crying. I could hardly bear to look at the photos of the children, but I couldn't bear *not* to look either', writes one missionary whose children attended boarding school.

'There have been many times when I have felt I am failing my children because I haven't fully understood what is going on, so I haven't been able to prepare them for what's going to happen, (Like) the time Julie and Paul arrived at a Father's Day event just as it was finishing because we hadn't understood . . .' writes another missionary.

Yet another missionary tells how well-meaning Christians at home challenged them about putting their children through hardships, separation and emotional upheaval—all because of their 'calling'.

Another writes; 'I cried that day, too, for a little boy who had had a disproportionate share of goodbyes in his life simply because he was a missionary's kid. Family and friends had come and gone in his life, and now the only pet he'd ever had also joined that ever-growing list'.

One mother shared how hard it was to see her kids struggling. She had known it would be difficult for herself—but to see her kids suffering! Your children may struggle with language. They may find it hard to play with other kids. They may be lonely or bullied. They may act up under the stress of change. But there can be other, more personal, challenges, too. Like the temptation to hide behind your children in order to avoid making the effort to build relationships or attend certain events or becoming so busy in ministry, you neglect your kids.

What can help you to travel through this minefield?

1   'From everyone who has been given much, much will be demanded . . .' (Luke 12:48b).

Perhaps surprisingly, this was God's word given to the anguished missionary whose children were far away in boarding school. However, that couple realised that they had indeed been given so much when they considered the hopelessness of those around them without Christ. How easy it is to get dragged in to the mud of self-pity, thinking how unfair God is to demand so much. Romans 8:32 helps put matters in perspective; 'He who did not spare his own Son, but gave him up for us all—how will he not also, along with him, graciously give us all things?'

2   'My children belong to God before they belong to me'.

These are the words that resonate with the missionary who was challenged about how their calling affected their kids. Even with all the advances in medicine, the reality is that God alone gives or with-holds the gift of children. Therefore, your children, like everything else in your life, belong to God first and you second. When Jesus talked about the cost of being a disciple, he said; 'If anyone comes to me and does not hate father and mother, wife and children, brothers and sisters—yes, even their own life—such a person cannot be my disciple . . . In the same way, those of you who do not give up every-thing you have cannot be my disciples' (Luke 14:26, 33).

One church planter was criticised for moving his family from suburbia to a rundown inner-city estate in London. When he prayed, he got this clear answer from God; 'Your son won't thank you if you don't obey me'. The cost to your children of your disobedience to God will always be greater than the price of your obedience.

3 'He tends his flock like a shepherd: he gathers the lambs in his arms and carries them close to his heart; he gently leads those that have young' (Isaiah 40:11).

The missionary mum whose daughter went to the Father's Day event at the wrong time treasures these words. Focus on the verbs in this verse—tends, gathers, carries and leads. Not only do these words illustrate God's care of us in every way, but our Good Shepherd doesn't simply carry, he carries us *close to his heart!* He doesn't just lead, he leads us *gently!* What comfort these words bring. God cares for you and he cares for your children. Even when you fail or are inadequate, even if your children are suffering and struggling with a new culture and language, God knows and God cares—far more than you ever could.

Interact

1 What challenges are facing you and your family at the moment? Write a list and talk to God about them.
2 Meditate on Luke 12:48b—what does that mean for you in your current situation?
3 Do you need to confess your sins of possessiveness or self-pity? Do so, knowing God longs to forgive and make you clean.
4 Write a list of all that God has given you and praise him!
5 Meditate on Matthew 19:27–30. Cry out to God in your pain and worship him for his goodness.
6 Take some time to deliberately hand back your children to God. If you feel you aren't able to do that yet, ask God to help you to be able to do it.
7 Have you been letting your kids become an excuse for poor language learning, relationship building or other things? Confess that to God and plan how you can balance your children and ministry needs.
8 Have you been letting your ministry squeeze out time with your kids? Confess that to God and make some concrete plans to spend time with your kids.

9   Meditate on Isaiah 40:11. Try putting your own name or the names of your kids in to this verse, and receive God's comfort and assurance.

Prayer

Thank you, Heavenly Father, that you gave up Jesus for me, and not just for me but for the whole world! Help me to focus every day on your sacrifice, so that I will get my perspective right. Help me to joyfully give my life, my family and my possessions in your service—I need help with that. I can't even begin to do it without you! Please help me balance my family and ministry needs and help me to encourage my spouse in these areas, too. But, Lord, thank you so much for being my Good Shepherd. Thank you that you carry me and my family close to your heart and that you promise to lead us gently. Lord, please care for my kids in ways I cannot even begin to. In Jesus' name, amen.

Family—in Your Home Country

*A*s a new missionary, Lucy rang her parents, using Skype, every couple of days. She loved to share her new life with them. Dave, a short-term missionary, spent the evenings chatting with his fiancée. Great, you might say—what's wrong with that? Or what about Lisa who came to the field and then made several trips to her home country within her first year? Is that OK—if your home country is close enough to do it? Why shouldn't it be OK? On the flip side, take Brenda, who was so busy that she struggled to keep in touch with folks at home. She was fulfilled in her work and used by God through her ministry. That's OK isn't it? That's what she came for after all. But when it came to home assignment, Brenda wasn't keen.

The truth is that having good relationships with family, friends and supporters in our home countries is vital to any missionary. The question is; how do we maintain those relationships as well as settle down in our field of service *and* build relationships with those in our local area—both Christian and non-Christian?

For those with reliable electricity supplies and ready Internet access, knowing just how often and how exactly to relate to people at home can be challenging. We have so many options at our finger-tips! Skype, Facebook, WhatsApp, e-mail—the list just goes on and on. However, if you are reading this in a place where electricity and Internet access are poor and intermittent, you will have a different set of challenges. How can you ensure that you keep in touch *enough*, with whom and how? Is it back to 'snail mail' for you?

And what about visits to or from family and friends? How often should we see those from 'home'? Is every year OK or too often? Should we go there? What about them coming here? In these days of quick and easy global travel, visits to or from family and friends can often become an issue for missionaries in ways it never used to be when C. T. Studd, Hudson Taylor, William Cameron Townsend and the like set off for foreign shores!

What can help us as we think through our relationships with those at home?

1   Hate Your Father and Mother!

'If anyone comes to me and does not hate father and mother, wife and children, brothers and sisters—yes, even their own life—such a person cannot be my disciple' (Luke 14:26). Jesus' words are a challenge to any Christian, but perhaps they resonate especially with overseas mission partners.

Jesus uses strong language here. In comparison to our love for Jesus, we are to be those who 'hate' our families! Everything and everyone who is precious to us must be thrown away rather than lose Jesus. In his commentary on this verse, Matthew Henry (7) says; 'When our duty to our parents comes in competition with our evident duty to Christ, we must give Christ the preference'.

You may have already made the sacrifice of leaving your home country and your family and friends in a literal, physical sense, but have you said goodbye figuratively and emotionally for the sake of the gospel?

2   Honour Your Father and Mother

'Honour your father and your mother, so that you may live long in the land the LORD your God is giving you' (Exodus 20:12). This verse perhaps gives the counterbalance to Jesus's words in Luke. We are to be those that honour our father and mother—and presumably the rest of our family, as well as our friends and supporters. The Christian gospel is about showing Christ's love to the world and that needs to include those close to us. John 19:27 also tells us about

Jesus' concern for his mum. In the midst of the excruciating pain of his death, Jesus says to John, 'Here is your mother'. The verse continues; 'From that time on, this disciple took her into his home'.

Simply because we are missionaries, it doesn't and can't mean that we have no responsibility of care toward our parents or other family members. However, we need to balance this with being willing to give up even family for the sake of Jesus and his kingdom.

Interact

1 Meditate on Luke 14:26. Are you a grudging or contented disciple in this area? Talk to Jesus about it and consider his example and how much pain that must have caused his family.
2 Practically, what does it mean for you, at this time, to honour your father and mother?
3 Think through your current relationships with family, friends, supporters and your home church. Consider how much time you spend maintaining those relationships, and how you do that? Is it insufficient or too much? About right? Confess any sinful actions to God.
4 Plan how you are going to move forward in this challenging area within the next year.
5 Think through how you use the Internet, if appropriate.
6 Think through your relationships with local people—how can you work toward strengthening those relationships?
7 How often do you see your family, friends or supporters? Is it about right, not enough or could it interfere with your ministry? Talk to God about it.
8 Do you need to make decisions or plans regarding care for your parents now or in the future?

Prayer

Lord Jesus, thank you that you gave up heaven and your close relationship with the Father—for me. Thank you, too, for the example you gave of sacrificing your earthly home life, as well as caring for your mum even as you were dying in agony on the cross. Please help me to get the right balance of honouring my family and those close to me, while at the same time putting you and your kingdom in your rightful place in my life—first. I pray this for your sake and the sake of your kingdom, amen.

Loneliness

A single missionary friend once told me how hard it was not to have anyone to do things with on a day off. Can you relate to that? Perhaps you are married, but you miss your girl or guy friends from your home country. No marriage partner—no matter how wonderful they are—can or should fulfil our every need for human companionship.

Other single friends have told me how some well-meaning Christians can treat singleness as a disease to be avoided. Some have been told, 'There's someone out there for you', or 'Your time will come'. Several single missionaries in Japan have been approached by caring friends to arrange a formal marriage interview for them, not uncommon among believers in Japan. Yet another single missionary was asked several times, 'When did you take a vow to remain single?' Her tongue-in-cheek reply was 'Maybe next year!'

I, too, can remember times of great loneliness as a new missionary. Your social circle is drastically reduced. You are new, in a brand new place, knowing virtually no one. You can't speak the language and don't understand the culture.

However, feelings of loneliness don't just come to singles, or new missionaries, they can come to anyone at any point in their missionary career. It may be that you are lonely as a leader. It may be that you are lonely because your close friend has moved to another part of the country, gone on home assignment or left the mission. Missionary life can often be a long round of hellos and goodbyes, which may result in feelings of loneliness.

What can we do?

> Do not be anxious about anything, but in every situation, by prayer and petition, with thanksgiving, present your requests to God. And the peace of God, which transcends all understanding, will guard your hearts and your minds in Christ Jesus. (Philippians 4:6–7)

These verses remind us that the peace of God comes not because of a change in our situation but because of a change in our hearts and minds through our trust in God and his working in us. You might be married and lonely; you might be single and lonely; you might be a new missionary and lonely or you might have been 'round the block a few times' and lonely! Whatever life situation we find ourselves in, we need to bring our loneliness to God 'by prayer and petition, with thanksgiving.' If we follow Paul's advice, we too *will* receive—it doesn't say that we *might* receive—the peace of God that transcends all understanding.

'For he satisfies the thirsty and fills the hungry with good things' (Psalm 107:9). Have you ever felt really thirsty? Northern Japan has very long, dry and cold winters; and because of the dryness of the atmosphere, you need to be careful to drink enough. I can remember many occasions when my throat felt parched, and then I felt the relief of cool clean water sliding down my throat! In the same way God is able to satisfy our thirst—whatever that thirst is for. One single missionary friend asked God to fulfil this promise in her life and little by little—over a period of time—she realised that he had done so. We worship a God who has given us all things! He has given us life, health, work, friends, families, and sometimes a marriage partner. Surely this God is also able to satisfy the thirsty and fill the hungry with good things!

Finally, especially for singles

> Now to the unmarried and the widows I say: it is good for them to stay unmarried, as I do . . . An unmarried man is concerned about the Lord's affairs—how he can please the Lord . . . An unmarried woman or

virgin is concerned about the Lord's affairs: her aim
is to be devoted to the Lord in both body and spirit .
. . I am saying this for your own good, not to restrict
you, but that you may live in a right way in undivided
devotion to the Lord. (1 Corinthians 7:8, 32, 34–35)

Several single missionary friends have commented to me how
much they would like to marry, but that they have found freedom in
being single and in embracing their singleness as a gift of God — on
a daily basis. One said, 'If God provides, praise Him. But regardless,
I want my life to be spent single-mindedly serving Him' Another
said, 'There is a freedom and a peace that comes from knowing
that where I am, is where God would have me for now, and that it
might change — or not'. Last, another said, 'This liberty to live where
God leads me without having to struggle with family ties has been a
blessing . . . I cannot think that it would have been so easy to make
all these changes had I been married or had dependent children. So I
praise God for his choice and that he has kept me faithful'.

Interact

1   Cry your feelings of loneliness out to God. It might be because
     you miss your friends from home, or because you don't have
     many friends in your host country, or because you are single
     and long to be married. Whatever it is, be honest before the
     Lord and grieve as you need to.
2   Present your requests to God. God wants to hear from you.
3   Meditate on Psalm 107.
4   Ask God to fill your heart and mind with his peace and to sat-
     isfy your hunger and thirst, even in the midst of your feelings
     of loneliness.
5   List practical steps you can take on a daily or weekly basis,
     which could help you build stronger relationships with those
     around you.
6   Whether you are married or single, how can you practically
     reach out to encourage others who may be struggling with
     loneliness?

Prayer

Thank you, Jesus, that you know what it's like to be lonely. When you faced death, all your friends deserted you. They couldn't even stay awake to pray with you, and when the end came, you were alone — even your Father turned his face away from you. Thank you that you understand. Lord, I am so lonely. I need your help. Please give me your peace and guard my heart. Please satisfy my thirst and fill my hunger with good things. Please use me for the sake of the gospel. Use even my need for friendship as a means of reaching others for your Kingdom. Lord, help me to have the courage to build strong friendships and help me to care for others who may also be lonely. In your name I pray, amen.

When Someone Dies

T write this the day after attending the funeral of a missionary couple's child. It was and continues to be simply heart-rending. There are no words. Another new worker finally makes it to the field, only to see their mother or father's condition deteriorate rapidly before they pass away. Being far away from home and loved ones at times like this is excruciating. A missionary on your field discovers they have cancer. They get all the treatment they can, but it's no good. They get weaker, usually they return to their home country, and they go to be with Jesus.

Death is painful wherever, whenever and however it happens. Death is the enemy. 'The last enemy to be destroyed is death' (1 Corinthians 15:26). Death hurts. However, one of the biggest struggles with death comes when we can't understand why. Why did that person suffer a miscarriage? Why did they have to die riddled with cancer? It doesn't matter who we are or what our situation might be, we all struggle with 'why.' However, as missionaries perhaps we may also ask why this happened to someone who had sacrificed everything to follow Christ and to bring his good news to the world. Perhaps—to put it even more bluntly—we want to ask God; 'I gave up everything for you: why are you treating me like this?'

We do not and cannot know the mind of God. However, we can say that God is good and just, and all things really do work together for good for those who love him. God can and will use all situations to glorify his name. We must hold on to that truth, above all. An old hymn, quoted at one particularly tragic funeral I attended says,

'God shall alone the refuge be,
And comfort of my mind;
Too wise to be mistaken He,
Too good to be unkind.

In all His holy, sovereign will,
He is, I daily find,
Too wise to be mistaken still,
Too good to be unkind.

When sore afflictions on me lie,
He is (though I am blind)
Too wise to be mistaken, yea,
Too good to be unkind.

What though I can't his doings see,
Nor all his footsteps find–
Too wise to be mistaken He,
Too good to be unkind.

Hereafter He will make me know,
And I shall surely find,
He was too wise to err, and oh!
Too good to be unkind'.

Samuel Medley
(Can be sung to St. Peter Reinagle)

Along with affirming God's goodness, justice and kindness, we must also affirm his presence with us in the midst of our suffering. Paul tells us in Romans 8:38–39, 'For I am convinced that neither death nor life, neither angels nor demons, neither the present nor the future, nor any powers, neither height nor depth, nor anything else in all creation, will be able to separate us from the love of God that is in Christ Jesus our Lord'. Whether our feelings reflect it or not, God is not absent from us when we live with the reality of death. 'Even though I walk through the darkest valley, I will fear no evil, for you are with me; your rod and your staff, they comfort me' (Psalm 23:4). God is with us in our pain. Believe it. It's a fact.

God is good. God is just. God is wise. God is present. And God is victorious! 'He will swallow up death for ever. The Sovereign Lord will wipe away the tears from all faces; he will remove his people's disgrace from all the earth. The Lord has spoken' (Isaiah 25:8). 'He will wipe away every tear from their eyes. There will be no more death or mourning, or crying, or pain, for the old order things has passed away' (Revelation 21:4). Whatever your situation right now, you can know for certain that God has and will have the ultimate victory. Believe it—whether your feelings reflect it or not.

Interact

1   Is someone important to you close to death or simply getting older so that you begin to fear what will happen? Has someone close to you died recently? Talk to God about these things.

2   Think through your response if someone you love in your home country dies. Will you go home before they die (if possible)? Will you go home for the funeral? What sort of leave of absence is provided by your organisation? Talk this through with your family members and make any appropriate preparations.

3   Have you been asking the 'why' question? If so, that's OK. God understands. Talk to him about that. Pour out your soul in prayer or in your journal. God can take it.

4   Search the Bible for references to God's goodness, justice and wisdom. Write a poem or prayer of trust to him.

5   Is there someone who needs you to come alongside them in their grief—either in prayer and/or in practical ways?

Prayer

Thank you, Father, that you gave the life of your only Son so that I might be forgiven and be raised with Christ. Thank you that you know the pain of losing one you love. Thank you that you are with me in this dark valley of death. I do believe: but help my unbelief. Thank you Father that you are just, kind, wise and present, but most especially I thank you that you are victorious over death. Lord, help me to grieve in the light of your victory. Help me also to help others as they grieve. In the name of Jesus, amen.

Notes

1   Isobel Kuhn, *Green Leaf in Drought-time,* Moody Press, 1957, p. 90

2   Isobel Kuhn, *Green Leaf in Drought-time,* Moody Press, 1957, p. 94

3   Amy Carmichael *Fragments that Remain* (compiled by Bee Trehane), 1987 by The Dohnavur Fellowship. CLC Publications, e-book 2013

4   Susan Miller *After the Boxes are Unpacked*, 1998, a Focus on the Family book published by Tyndale House Publishers, Inc.

5   Helen Roseveare, *Give Me This Mountain,* IVP, 1966, p. 48

6   C. S. Lewis, *The Horse and His Boy,* Lions (HarperCollins), 1954, chapter 11

7   Matthew Henry *Matthew Henry's Commentary,* 1708–1710

Appendix

Dealing Positively with People I Find Difficult

First, I must deal with myself before God.

1) I will choose to remember who I am in Christ.

2) I will remember that I am deeply loved.

3) I will remember that I am totally secure.

4) I will remember that God loves me just as much as _____.

5) I will remember that being young and inexperienced doesn't mean I have to feel guilty or insecure.

6) I will choose to set my mind on what is right, on what God says about me.

7) I will ask myself who I am seeking to please—myself, God, my team members or team leaders, and so forth.

Second about other people . . .

1) I will encourage, support, praise and pray for my fellow team members and team leaders.

2) I will always choose to believe/remember that _____ is made and gifted by God.

3) I will always choose to remember that _____ is a godly person, trying their best to serve God.

4) I will always choose to trust that _____'s motives are good.

5) I will always choose to remember that when _____ outlines their idea, they don't expect it to start right away!

6) I will choose to be encouraging, not discouraging toward _____.

7) I will ask clarifying questions to ascertain for myself and for them, which direction we are thinking of going.

8) I will explain how I feel about the situation.

9) I will confront or disagree with _____ when necessary, with God's help and courage.

CPSIA information can be obtained
at www.ICGtesting.com
Printed in the USA
BVHW042146060620
580993BV00012B/1110

9 781498 470919